COUNTRIES
OF THE
WORLD

Mexico

Gareth Stevens Publishing
MILWAUKEE

Dr. Leslie Jermyn is a professional anthropologist who has done field research in both South and Central America. She has written largely for academic audiences but draws on her extensive teaching experience to inform her popular writing.

Written by
LESLIE JERMYN

Edited by
AYESHA ERCELAWN

Designed by
SHARIFAH FAUZIAH

Picture research by
SUSAN JANE MANUEL

First published in North America in 1998 by
Gareth Stevens Publishing
1555 North RiverCenter Drive, Suite 201
Milwaukee, Wisconsin 53212 USA

For a free color catalog describing
Gareth Stevens' list of high-quality books
and multimedia programs, call
1-800-542-2595 (USA)
1-800-461-9120 (CANADA)
Gareth Stevens Publishing's
Fax: (414) 225-0377
See our catalog, on the World Wide Web:
http://gsinc.com

© **TIMES EDITIONS PTE LTD 1998**
Originated and designed by
Times Books International
an imprint of Times Editions Pte Ltd
Times Centre, 1 New Industrial Road
Singapore 536196
http://www.timesone.com.sg/te

Library of Congress Cataloging-in-Publication Data
Jermyn, Leslie.
Mexico / by Leslie Jermyn.
p. cm. — (Countries of the world)
Includes bibliographical references and index.
Summary: Introduces the geography, history, economy, government, culture, food, and people of Mexico.
ISBN 0-8368-2127-0 (lib. bdg.)
1. Mexico — Juvenile literature. [1. Mexico] I. Title. II. Series: Countries of the world (Milwaukee, Wis.)
F1208.5.J47   1998
972—dc21   98-13771

Printed in Singapore

1 2 3 4 5 6 7 8 9 02 01 00 99 98

PICTURE CREDITS
A.N.A Press Agency: 12, 22, 23 (bottom), 48, 49, 54, 62, 63, 67
Andes Press Agency: 10, 20, 23 (top), 44 (top), 58 (both)
Bes Stock: 30
Camera Press Ltd: 84 (both)
Sylvia Cordaiy Photo Library: 83
Victor Englebert: 59
Ayesha Ercelawn: 51
Focus Team: 27 (bottom), 47 (top), 66
Dave G. Houser: 78 (bottom)
The Hutchison Library: 1, 2, 3 (top), 7, 19, 29, 32, 40, 42, 52, 64
The Image Bank: 17, 74
Life File Photo Library: 43, 46, 81
North Wind Picture Archives: 77 (top)
Photobank Photolibrary/Singapore: cover, 34, 91
David Simson: 3 (center), 5, 14, 21, 27 (top), 28 (both), 37, 47 (bottom), 60, 68
South American Pictures: 11, 15, 18, 35, 36, 39, 44 (bottom), 56, 61, 69, 70, 71, 73, 79, 82, 85
Tan Chung Lee: 13, 31, 41, 53, 72
Liba Taylor: 3 (bottom), 4, 8, 16, 38, 78 (top), 80
Times Editions: 50
Topham Picturepoint: 6, 9, 26, 33, 45, 65, 75, 77 (bottom)
Travel Ink: 25, 76
Trip Photographic Library: 24, 55, 57

Contents

AN OVERVIEW OF MEXICO

This book is about Mexico — its history, culture, geography, people, politics, and much more. The nation has a long and colorful history, from rule by powerful Indian empires, such as the Aztecs and Maya, to colonization by the Spanish. Today, Mexico has a thriving culture and language, with both Indian and Spanish influences. The population is mostly mestizo, people of mixed Spanish and Indian ancestry, although there are also pure Indian communities in the south. This book will take you on a richly varied tour to learn about Mexico's customs and its dramatic landscape.

Opposite: In villages, donkeys are a form of transportation for people and goods.

Below: The influence of Aztec Indian practices continues in Mexico today. In this performance at the Virgin of Guadalupe festival, young dancers wear Aztec costumes with feather headdresses.

THE FLAG OF MEXICO

The Mexican flag has three vertical bars of green, white, and red. Green symbolizes hope and fertility; white means purity; and red represents the blood lost during the war for independence from Spain. These three colors were established in 1821, at the time of Mexico's independence. On the white panel, there is a crest of an eagle sitting on top of a cactus and devouring a snake. The crest is a symbol from the Aztecs, a powerful Indian tribe, who according to legend were told by their god to locate their capital in the place where they saw an eagle eating a snake. They came across this site in 1325 and established Tenochtitlán, Mexico City today.

Geography

The Land

Mexico is the southernmost country of the North American continent. It covers a total area of 756,066 square miles (1,958,210 square kilometers) and has a population of approximately 87,341,000 people. The United States borders Mexico to the north, and Guatemala and Belize lie to the southeast. There is water on both sides of the country — the Gulf of California and the Pacific Ocean are to the west and south, and the Gulf of Mexico and the Caribbean Sea lie to the east.

Mexico is shaped like a big horn curving southeast and turning back on itself in the Yucatán Peninsula. Two chains of mountain ranges lie along the coasts — the Sierra Madre Occidental in the west and the Sierra Madre Oriental in the east. The narrowest part of the country in the south is called the Isthmus of Tehuantepec. The two ranges meet near the isthmus to form a mountainous region primarily populated by Indians.

Below: Mt. Popocatépetl is one of the highest volcanoes in Mexico. Its name means "smoking mountain" in the Nahuatl Indian language. It last erupted in 1702 and still occasionally releases huge clouds of smoke.

The Mexican Plateau lies in the middle of the country, between the two mountain ranges. Volcanic activity has shaped much of this area, and earthquakes still occur. It is also the most densely populated region of Mexico. The capital, Mexico City, is located in a valley here. The formerly great Indian civilizations were centered in this valley. It was also the most important area for Spanish settlement and continues so today.

The northern parts of the plateau are very dry, but the southern areas get more rainfall and are very fertile. The land slopes gently north toward the border with the United States. This border is partly formed by a river, the Río Bravo del Norte, known as the Rio Grande in the United States.

The Pacific Coastal Lowlands occupy a narrow strip of land between the Pacific Ocean and the Sierra Madre Occidental range. The southern lowlands are lush and include rain forest. In contrast, a long finger of land, Baja California, juts into the Pacific Ocean and is mostly semidesert or desert. In the east, the Gulf Coastal Plain borders the Gulf of Mexico down to the Yucatán Peninsula. It is mostly swampy areas and lagoons. The Yucatán Peninsula is a limestone plateau with tropical rain forest.

Above: **Much of Baja California is desert or semidesert, and it has more than one hundred and twenty species of cacti. The area is also famous for its lizards, including the Gila monster and the Mexican beaded lizard, both of which are poisonous.**

CACTUS AND CENTURY PLANTS

Prickly looking though they are, some cactus plants can be used by people. Both the leaves and fruit of certain species can be eaten and are said to be delicious!
(A Closer Look, page 46)

Seasons

More than half of Mexico lies in the tropics, which means hot weather all year. But the climate is also greatly influenced by altitude. The higher up in the mountains you go, the colder it gets. The hottest areas are the low-lying Yucatán Peninsula, the east coast, and the dry northern regions. In the Yucatán Peninsula, even winter temperatures stay high, around 75° Fahrenheit (24° Centigrade), and summer temperatures average 80° F (27° C). In the populated central Mexican Plateau, summer temperatures can be quite cool at higher elevations but warmer in lower areas. Winter temperatures can fall to nearly freezing.

Summer, from May to August, is the rainy season, but the amount of rain varies widely across the country. In Chiapas, in the south, there are areas that receive up to 200 inches (5,000 millimeters) of rain per year, while the northern deserts may get only 5–10 inches (125–250 mm) per year. In the central valleys, it rains almost every afternoon during this season. The west and east coasts average about 30 inches (750 mm) per year, while Yucatán gets about 60 inches (1,500 mm). The country experiences heavy tropical hurricanes on both coasts from August through October.

Below: **Millions of orange and black monarch butterflies cling to trees in Mexico's southern mountains. This is not only an incredible sight, but also an incredible sound, for the flutter of their wings can be heard when they reach these numbers. These butterflies spend summers in the United States and Canada, and then migrate 3,000–5,000 miles (5,000–8,000 km) every year to spend the winter in Mexico's southern mountains.**

Plants and Animals

Because of the diverse climate across the country, Mexico has many different ecosystems, each with its own collection of plants and animals. The broad central plain, between the mountains of the Sierra Madre Occidental and Oriental, is very dry and is covered with scrub plants like the prickly-pear cactus, mesquite, and agave (century plant). In the middle of the Chihuahua Desert, there are species of fish, living in natural springs, that exist nowhere else in the world. In the mountain lowlands, there are oaks, junipers, and piñon pines. Because few people live in this region, there is abundant wildlife, including rabbits, foxes, ringtail cats, coatimundi, wild turkeys, coyotes, and pumas.

Above: **Coatimundis are found in the jungles on the eastern coast of Mexico. They are about the size of raccoons and are active during the day. They have long snouts and eat plants, small animals, and insects.**

In contrast, the wetter areas near the Gulf of Mexico are covered in tropical rain forest. The forests around Chiapas and Oaxaca are home to opossums, armadillos, rabbits, porcupines, agoutis, jaguars, and ocelots. Swampier areas have turtles, alligators, and lizards.

The lowlands of Baja California are covered with small trees and bushes called chaparral, and much of the area is desert. Coyotes, black bears, and wolves hunt in Baja, while the waters off the coast are a winter haven for gray whales, harbor seals, and sea lions.

History

Indian Civilizations

Before the arrival of Europeans, Mexico was a land of many different Indian groups. Some were small agricultural societies, while others developed large city-states. Many Indian tribes, including the Maya, the Toltecs, and the Aztecs, became great powers. The Aztecs were a fierce group that established an empire stretching from coast to coast in Mexico by the early sixteenth century.

Spanish Rule, 1521–1821

Hernán Cortés, a Spaniard, landed in Mexico in 1519 with a few hundred troops. Joined by Indian tribes who were unhappy with Aztec rule, he defeated the Aztecs and by 1521, took over their capital city, Tenochtitlán. The colony became known as New Spain and was governed in the name of the Spanish king. New Spain eventually covered a huge territory, stretching from parts of present-day United States to the borders of Costa Rica in southern Central America.

THE AZTECS

The Aztecs were fierce warriors who had a large empire until they were conquered by the Spanish. Their capital was at Tenochtitlán, today's Mexico City.
(A Closer Look, page 44)

Below: This mosaic shows Montezuma, king of the Aztecs, in the center. He was defeated by Hernán Cortés, shown in armor on his horse.

10

Independence from Spain

Although it was the Indians who suffered the most under Spanish rule, the demand for independence came from Spaniards born in Mexico who wanted self-rule. On September 16, 1810, Miguel Hidalgo y Costilla, a priest in the town of Dolores (now Dolores Hidalgo), began the war for independence. He pulled together a small army of peasants, but was captured and executed by Spanish forces in 1811. For the next ten years, fighting in Mexico continued, under the leadership of Agustín de Iturbide. Finally, on August 24, 1821, General Iturbide convinced Spain's representative to sign the Treaty of Córdoba, which granted Mexico its freedom.

Benito Juárez and The Reform

For the next fifty-five years, the new country was very unstable. During the period known as The Reform (1855–1876), new laws took away special privileges of the Roman Catholic Church. This angered many people, and there was civil war from 1858 to 1860. Those wanting the changes won the war, and their leader, Benito Juárez, became president in 1860. Mexico endured a brief occupation by the French (1861–1867) during Juárez's presidency.

Above: **This large mural shows Father Hidalgo grasping the fire of rebellion. The mural was painted by José Clemente Orozco.**

THE SPANISH CONQUEST

Hernán Cortés led the Spanish conquest of the Aztec empire. The Aztecs, who had never seen white people or horses before, believed him to be a god.
(A Closer Look, page 62)

The Porfiriato, 1876–1910

Porfirio Díaz took over soon after the death of Juárez. The period of his repressive rule is known as the Porfiriato. Díaz tried to modernize Mexico by building railroads and encouraging foreign companies to invest money. Unfortunately, he did not support the causes he once fought for alongside Juárez. Large landowners were allowed to take even more land, and the poor got poorer. He did not allow anyone else to win elections and remained president eight times in a row. Eventually, many Mexicans got fed up with Díaz's policies and started a revolution in 1910 to get rid of him.

The Mexican Revolution, 1910–1920

Under the leadership of Emiliano Zapata and Francisco "Pancho" Villa, many peasants rose up against Díaz, as did some middle class groups. The rebellion that started in 1910 resulted in a civil war that killed 1.5 million Mexicans and sent a million more into exile in the United States. It finally ended with an election in 1920 that re-established normal government and put new leaders in power.

MEXICAN–AMERICAN WAR

The Mexican–American War took place between 1846 and 1848. Mexico had to give up more than half its territory, including present day Texas, New Mexico, and California, to the United States.

Below: Emiliano Zapata was an important peasant leader during the Mexican Revolution.

The Twentieth Century

The revolution shaped Mexico's future. One of the reasons for the war had been the harsh life of poor peasants. The government has since tried to improve their lives by giving them more land. Over the years since the revolution, Mexico has made great efforts to educate and provide health services for its growing population. This has not always been easy because the population of Mexico has increased very quickly, and many of these people have moved from the countryside into the cities looking for work. Sadly, the number of jobs has not increased as quickly as the number of people looking for work. This means that the cities, especially Mexico City, are filled with poor people with no chance of finding work or housing. The people who stay in the country are also having a hard time making a living because they still do not have enough land to farm.

Mexico has been headed by Ernesto Zedillo Ponce de León since 1994. He is part of the dominant political party, the Institutional Revolutionary Party (PRI) and faces many difficult challenges during the six years of his term. Educated as an economist at Yale University in the United States, he has done more than any of his recent predecessors to bring democracy and honest elections to Mexico.

Above: **The village of San Juán Chamula. While many rural people are moving to the cities, others remain in their small towns and villages and continue to follow traditional ways of life.**

¡VIVA ZAPATA!

On January 1, 1994, a group of Indians in Chiapas state started a rebellion. Many of them are very poor and want work, food, housing, education, and better health care. They call themselves the Zapatista National Liberation Army, after Emiliano Zapata.

(A Closer Look, page 70)

13

Father Hidalgo

Although Miguel Hidalgo y Costilla did not live to see Mexican independence in 1821, he has an important place in history because he started the war against Spain. He attended university in Mexico City and later became a priest. In 1803, he was transferred to the town of Dolores, where he worked hard to help the local people. He started a number of factories to help the poor get work. He also learned the local Indian languages, which was rare for Mexico's religious leaders at the time. Because Hidalgo was so popular with the Indians, he was able to gather hundreds of people together to help him fight. His untrained army mostly had to fight with simple weapons and farm tools. The armies defending Spain eventually captured and killed Father Hidalgo, but he lives on in Mexican memory as the Father of Independence.

Benito Juárez (1806–1872)

Juárez is best known for his actions as president of Mexico from 1858 to 1872. He supported changes that took some of the power away from the Catholic Church, and he resisted French attempts to take over Mexico. He was the first Indian to play such a major role in

Below: Mexico was invaded by the French while Benito Juárez was president. Mexico had stopped making payments to European countries on loans it could not meet. This gave the French the excuse they were looking for, and in 1861, under Napoleon III, they started a war with Mexico. Juárez and his men fought hard and finally kicked the French out in 1867.

independent Mexico, and his story is that of a true hero. He was born near Oaxaca to Zapotec Indian parents. Both his parents died when he was only four years old. He lived with relatives and worked in the fields until the age of twelve. When he decided to get an education, he walked to Oaxaca to live with his sister and try to go to school. A monk who lived in town decided to help him. Although Juárez knew only a little Spanish, he managed to learn Latin! By 1834, he finished law school and started his career in politics. He held a number of important positions in Oaxaca state and in the federal government, and was president of Mexico for fourteen years. He died in 1872 and has been considered a national hero ever since.

"Pancho" Villa (1878–1923)

Francisco "Pancho" Villa was a popular rural leader in the Mexican Revolution of 1910. He joined the call to revolution with a band of fighters in the northern state of Chihuahua and combined forces with Emiliano Zapata. After the revolution, he continued fighting from northern Mexico. He was killed on his ranch in 1923. Today, he is remembered as a legend.

Government and the Economy

Government

The current constitution of the United States of Mexico was proclaimed in 1917 and is the result of the 1910 revolutionary struggle against Porfirio Díaz. The revolution started because Mexicans were tired of extreme inequality between the rich and poor and of dictators who stayed in power without democratic support. The constitution divides and limits power among three governmental branches — the executive, legislative, and judicial. The executive branch of government is headed by the president. The president approves the laws made by the legislative branch and can make independent decisions in some financial and economic areas. There is a presidential election once every six years, and every adult is allowed to vote. Once someone has been president, they can never run for election to this office again.

Below: **A political rally in the main plaza of Mexico City. This plaza, the *zócalo* (SO-kah-loh), is the second largest in the world and has been a public square since the time of the Aztecs. The National Cathedral (on the left) and the National Palace (right) are both located here. The National Palace houses the offices of the president of Mexico, the National Archives, and the Federal Treasury.**

The legislative branch is divided into a senate and a chamber of deputies, which together form the Congress. There are 500 deputies, and the senate is composed of 128 senators.

Above: **A military parade in Mexico City.**

The judicial branch is divided into federal- and state-level courts. The federal courts deal with cases involving national law and the constitution. Major criminal cases may also be tried in the federal circuit courts. The Supreme Court has twenty-one regular members and five special ones appointed by the president. State courts deal with minor crimes and state laws. Criminal cases are tried only by a judge, not a jury.

Political Parties

The main political party in Mexico is the Partido Revolucionario Institucional (PRI) or Institutional Revolutionary Party. The PRI has won every presidential election since it was formed. Mexico is not a one-party state, however, and other parties are allowed to run candidates for election. To be considered a legitimate political party, a group must win 1.5 percent of the vote in two consecutive elections. This shows they are popular enough to be a political party. The strongest opposition parties today are the National Action Party (PAN) and the Revolutionary Democratic Party (PRD). The first is more conservative than the PRI, while the second is more liberal.

Natural Resources

In 1974, oil and natural gas reserves were discovered in eastern Mexico. Mexico supplies all its own gas and oil needs and is also a major exporter. It is the world's fifth largest producer of oil. Mexico also has significant mineral resources and is a leading exporter of silver, sulfur, lead, and zinc. There are also gold, copper, manganese, coal, and iron-ore mines.

Agriculture

Agriculture is divided between small farms that produce food for their own household and large farms that primarily produce crops for export. Since the revolution, the government has been trying to ensure that every farmer has enough land to grow food for the family. This has been very difficult, however, because there is not enough agricultural land in the country. Many farmers have such small plots they have to find additional ways to earn money. The other problem is that before the revolution, huge areas of land were owned by just a few rich landowners. It has not been easy for the government to take it away from them and distribute it to poorer farmers.

Below: Children usually help in the fields in rural areas. Here, they are harvesting sugarcane, one of Mexico's main export crops. The other major export crops are coffee, cotton, fruit, and vegetables (especially tomatoes). Corn, wheat, sorghum, barley, rice, and beans are also grown. In northern Mexico, where the land is very dry, there are many cattle ranches.

Industry

Mexico has an important manufacturing sector. About one-fifth of the economy and workers are involved in factory production. Cars, chemicals, processed food products, drinks, and electrical machinery are manufactured. About half of the manufacturing sector is made up of *maquiladoras* (mah-kee-lah-DOHR-ahs), small factories located along the Mexico–U.S. border.

Above: **Men work on an oil rig. Oil production was nationalized in Mexico in the 1930s.**

Trade

Mexico's main trading partner is the United States. About 63 percent of Mexico's imports come from the United States, and about 68 percent of its exports go there. Since 1994, Canada, the United States, and Mexico have been part of a special trade agreement called the North American Free Trade Agreement (NAFTA). NAFTA is basically a plan to make trading easier among these three countries. Other important trading partners for Mexico are Japan, Spain, France, Germany, and Brazil. Although Mexico is much poorer than the United States, it has many valuable resources, and its government is working hard to improve economic conditions for all Mexicans.

People and Lifestyle

Who Are the Mexicans?

The population of modern Mexico is a mixture of Spanish and Indian ancestry. Spanish settlers and Indians lived very separate lives at first, but slowly, throughout the colonial period, Spanish men started marrying Indian women. Their children were called mestizos, and they make up the majority of the Mexican population today. There are also many different Indian groups in Mexico.

Mestizos

Mestizos are the dominant cultural group. Their values and beliefs resemble European-based cultures more than Indian ones. The main distinctions within the mestizo group are those of wealth and occupation. The wealthy still have large estates, even after the revolution. Those who do not have enough land or have none at all work for large landowners, or they go to the cities to find jobs. However, there are not enough jobs in the cities. The urban poor often have to live in shantytowns without water or sewers. In contrast, the rich can afford modern houses and a good education.

MEXICO CITY

Mexico City is Mexico's capital and cultural center. The crowded city draws many people from rural areas looking for jobs, but serious urban problems these days include terrible air pollution, a lack of water, and frequent earthquakes. *(A Closer Look, page 56)*

Below: **Many Mexicans have a mix of Spanish and Indian blood.**

Left: **In the Mexican countryside, many people have barely enough land to make a living. Poor families may work on land owned by others, and they depend on all their family members, including the children, to work.**

Indians

Many Indian communities in Mexico are rural and fairly isolated. They include the Yaqui, the Maya, the Zapotec, the Mixtec, and Nahuatl-speaking descendants of the Aztecs. These groups managed to stay free of direct Spanish control and retained most of their cultural practices, although this has been changing over the last fifty years. They have their own gods and religious beliefs, speak Indian languages rather than Spanish, and are primarily poor farmers growing just enough food for themselves. The focus of life is mainly the local community, not the wider world.

Family Life

All Mexicans believe in the importance of family. The whole family often eats the midday meal together, and Sundays are days for family gatherings. Generally, the husband is considered the head of the household, and women are expected to stay home to care for their husband and children. This is changing in urban areas, where more women are working before and after marriage, but a working mother is still an exception among middle class households. Grandparents are deeply respected for their age and wisdom, and sometimes three generations live together in one house.

Godparents

Most Mexicans also have godparents, *compadres* (kom-PAH-drays). These are people who agree to serve as a second set of parents at the baptism of a new baby. They help the parents pay for the celebration and continue to help the child as he or she grows up. In Mexico, the relationship goes both ways — the child may also be asked to help the godparents in times of need. The compadre system in Mexico is unique because people may have

Below: **This Sunday picnic includes the extended family. They are picnicking among fields of agave and have also brought their own musicians along.**

many sets of godparents, one set for each special occasion in their lives. So, in addition to having godparents for the baptism, there may be different godparents who help with the wedding celebrations or school graduation celebrations. These types of relationships connect many non-related people together through mutual help and concern.

From Baptism to Marriage

There are three very important ceremonies that Mexicans celebrate in their life: baptism, *quince años* (KEEN-say AHN-yos) for girls, and marriage. Baptism in the Catholic Church marks the time when a baby becomes a new member of society. Quince años, meaning fifteen years, is a special celebration for girls on their fifteenth birthday. If the family can afford it, the girl will be given a special party with all her friends and friends of the family. She usually wears a white dress and gets gifts from her guests.

All young men and women are expected to marry and have children. Mexico is quite traditional in this sense. Girls in rural areas often marry at a young age — between the ages of fourteen and sixteen.

Top: **This bride and groom are riding on horseback through the streets of Mexico City!**

Above: **Children are usually confirmed in the Catholic Church between the ages of eleven and thirteen. Girls wear new, white dresses for the occasion.**

Education

At the time of the revolution in 1910, Mexico had an illiteracy rate of 80 percent, but now it is down to 13 percent. Since the revolution, the government has worked hard to improve access to primary and secondary education. Primary school (grades one to six) is free, and school attendance is compulsory for all children aged six to fourteen years or until they complete all grades. Secondary school is free but not compulsory and lasts for another six years. In 1992, all children of primary school age were attending school, but only 56 percent of those old enough for secondary school were enrolled.

State universities are also free, and there are private universities as well. The enrollment of students increased dramatically from 62,000 students in 1959, to 1.5 million by 1990. The king of Spain started the first university in Mexico in 1551, the Royal University in Mexico City.

There are many problems that make it difficult to provide an education for everyone. Poverty is widespread, both in cities and villages. The government has worked hard to build and improve rural schools, but many families simply cannot afford to send their children. Although school is free, children must also have supplies, textbooks, and uniforms. These are especially difficult for poor farmers to provide because they do not have much cash on hand.

Below: **Children study in the Spanish language at school. Many attend only primary school, but Mexico has been investing large amounts of money in its educational system.**

Left: **Many families cannot afford to send their children to school. Instead, the children are needed to help earn extra money for the family. This girl in Mexico City plays the accordion for passersby, hoping to earn some money.**

Another problem is that the poorest families depend on everyone, even the youngest, to contribute to the family income. In rural areas, children often help on the farm, while in cities they may be seen begging when they should be in school. Another problem some children face is language. Mexican education is in Spanish only, but among the more isolated Indian communities, most children only know their native language. This makes it very difficult for them since they must first learn Spanish before they can learn math or other subjects. Imagine if you had to learn a new language in order to go to school! These problems will not be solved overnight, but the government continues to devote a large part of its annual budget to making it easier for children to go to primary school.

Left: **This magnificent carving of the serpent god, Quetzalcoatl, is found on one of the temples at Teotihuacán, outside Mexico City.**

The Aztec Gods

Before the arrival of Europeans, there were many different religions in the area now called Mexico. Each Indian culture had its own gods and goddesses and its own set of religious practices. Many of the great civilizations believed in blood sacrifice to the gods. The Aztecs even offered human hearts to the Sun God to help him continue to burn. Many of the Indian peasants still hold traditional beliefs today, sometimes side by side with Roman Catholic practices.

One of the Aztec gods, Quetzalcoatl, was quite important to the Spanish conquest. His name in Nahuatl means "quetzal-feathered snake." The quetzal is a beautiful jungle bird with long, green feathers that lives throughout Central America. Quetzalcoatl was the god of wind and breath, both symbols of fertility, and he was thought to be a snake covered with the quetzal's feathers. The Aztecs believed that he would some day come to their city from the east in human form. When Hernán Cortés landed on the east coast of Mexico, the Aztecs believed he was Quetzalcoatl because he looked so different from themselves, with his fair skin and shiny metal armor. Some historians think this is why the conquest of the Aztecs was so easy — the Aztecs were afraid of angering their god.

MAGIC IN MEXICO

Only a special healer can cure people of illnesses such as the "evil eye." In rural areas, where Christianity and Indian religions have fused, a healer may use special herbs, chant, or pray to one of the saints to cure a sick person.

(A Closer Look, page 54)

Christianity

Today, 94 percent of Mexicans are Roman Catholic. The first Franciscan missionaries arrived in 1524, only three years after the conquest of the Aztecs. They started schools to teach the Indians Spanish and to convert them to Catholicism. The Catholic Church became very powerful in Mexico and was the largest landowner until the revolution.

Catholicism in Mexico is a blend of Indian and European ideas. The early missionaries found it easier to persuade the Indians to come to church if some of the rituals and saints appeared more like traditional Indian practices. For example, the Catholic observance of Day of the Dead is not common outside Mexico, but it became very popular there because it is similar to Aztec rituals for their dead. People also offer sacrifices to Catholic saints as if they were Aztec gods. In small village churches, saints may have mirrors around their necks to reflect the sun god of Aztec times.

There has been a new wave of missionary work among Mexico's Indians in recent years. This time, the missionaries are from Protestant evangelical churches in North America. In some rural areas of Mexico, up to one-third of the population has converted. This form of Protestantism has appeal because it does not allow the drinking of alcohol, a widespread problem among the poor. Protestantism also helps its believers escape from the village hierarchy and the associated expenses of religious festivals.

THE VIRGIN OF GUADALUPE

The Virgin Mary is special to many Mexicans. Legend has it that she appeared as an Indian woman to a poor peasant near Guadalupe. Since then, she has become an important symbol for all Mexicans. There is a special feast day for her, and a church in Guadalupe has her image on a cape.
(*A Closer Look, page 68*)

Left: Most Mexicans are Roman Catholic. Missionaries from Spain converted the local people to Catholicism, and many beautiful churches were built throughout the country. This lavishly gilded and carved Church of Santo Domingo was built in Puebla in 1690.

Language and Literature

Spanish

Most people in Mexico speak Spanish. People in different regions of the country speak with different accents and use different local expressions. The country can be divided into three main regions according to the dialect spoken in each — Chilango is spoken in south-central Mexico including Mexico City; Norteño Spanish is spoken in northern Mexico along the border with the United States; and Yucateco Spanish is used in the Yucatán area. People include Mayan words in their Spanish in the Yucatán.

In northern Mexico, English words have been "Mexicanized" so that lunch is *lonche* (LOHN-chay); home run is *jonrón* (hon-ROHN); and the verb to park a car is *parquear* (par-kay-AHR). These words may not look familiar in Spanish, but if you say them out loud, they sound very much like the English words.

Indian Languages

The national language of Mexico is Spanish, but there are also as many as fifty native Indian languages still spoken in isolated parts of the country. Nahuatl, the language of the Aztec state, has been the most important in the history of Mexico. Early Spanish traders, settlers, and missionaries used Nahuatl as a common language to communicate. Many of the words for food and cooking in Spanish today actually come from Nahuatl: for example, *tamale* (tah-MAH-lay), *tortilla* (tor-TEE-yaa), *comal* (KOH-mahl), and *metate* (may-TAH-tay).

Above: Toros (TOH-rohs), or bulls, can be seen fighting every Wednesday according to this billboard.

MEXICO'S FAMOUS WRITERS

Laura Esquivel, a Mexican writer, has become internationally famous for her book, *Like Water for Chocolate*, now also a movie. Other Mexican writers are also popular within and outside of Mexico.
(*A Closer Look*, page 58)

Left: This newspaper stand is selling a range of newspapers in Spanish.

Place Names

Many place names in Mexico come from Indian languages. For example, the name Mexico itself comes from the Aztecs. Similarly, Oaxaca, Zacatecas, and Taxco come from Indian words. The names of some American states also come from Mexican-Indian words: Texas and New Mexico! The reason is that these states belonged to Mexico until the Mexican–American War.

Mexican Literature

Mexico has a long tradition of great writers. Perhaps the best known book written about Mexico is *The Discovery and Conquest of Mexico* by Bernal Díaz. He was a Spanish priest who accompanied Hernán Cortés on his first mission to the New World. Díaz was very observant, and his writings are our best source for understanding how native people lived around the time of the conquest. More recently, the translations of Mexican writers such as Octavio Paz and Carlos Fuentes have become quite famous among English-speaking readers. Other well known writers are Elena Poniatowska, María Luisa Puga, and Laura Esquivel.

Above: People in Mexico speak different dialects of Spanish in different regions. Various Indian languages are also still alive. In southeastern Mexico, on the Yucatán Peninsula, Mayan is still spoken by many people as a first language, especially in rural areas. Other Indian languages that survive today include Zapotecan, Mixtecan, Totonacan, Huastecan, Otomí, Tarrascan, and Yaqui.

Arts

Art and architecture in Mexico are a combination of native Indian styles and European styles introduced during the colonial period. Both influences have created a distinctive art form that draws on the symbols and techniques of the great pre-Columbian civilizations as well as the European colonial heritage.

Pre-Columbian Art

The great civilizations of Mexico — the Aztecs, Teotihuacán people, Toltec, Olmec, and Maya — all had their own distinctive styles of sculpture and painting. Images of pre-Christian gods and spirits, such as the Jaguar and Quetzalcoatl, were carved into stone sculptures. Late civilizations, like the Aztecs, made gold and silver masks and ornaments decorated with semiprecious stones, such as turquoise. A common element of pre-conquest art was brightly colored wall paintings, or murals. Murals decorated the sacred sites and even simple houses of Tenochtitlán. The nobility of these civilizations wore beautiful capes made of feathers and intricately woven and embroidered clothes. Dancers wore elaborate masks.

Below: **The pyramid form was used in many of the great cities that flourished before the Spaniards arrived. This is one of the temples in the city of Teotihuacán, the capital of a sophisticated civilization until the eighth century A.D. It was abandoned for unknown reasons.**

Spanish Colonial Architecture

The Spanish at first destroyed much of the native culture, tearing down temples and forcing Indians to become Christian. By the late colonial period, in the 1700s, a new, uniquely New World architectural style called Churrigueresque emerged. It is similar to Baroque art. Both styles feature complicated stone and wood carvings with many swirling, intertwined images. Mexico City's main cathedral is a good example of the Baroque style, while Zacatecas and Taxco have Churrigueresque style churches.

A New, Post-Revolutionary Style

Indian and Spanish traditions came together in the twentieth century, after the Mexican Revolution. The revolution was very important artistically because it signaled Mexico's break with colonialism and the poor treatment of Indian people. Artists started to include many of the forms of the great Indian civilizations in their work, to show that Mexican identity was both European and Indian. The new state was the biggest patron of the arts, and many public buildings were created in this new style.

Above: **This cathedral at Zacatecas has an elaborately carved facade, with saints, columns, and many decorations, all in the Churrigueresque style of architecture.**

TAXCO: TOWN OF SILVER

Taxco has been an important silver town for many years. In the 1930s, William Spratling, an American, settled in Taxco and started designing silver jewelry in ancient Indian motifs. His pieces became immensely popular.
(A Closer Look, page 64)

Music

Music is a very important part of Mexican life, and every celebration includes musicians. The most commonly heard musical style is the *norteña* (nor-TAYN-ya). This music includes influences from European polkas, waltzes, Mexican ballads, and salsa! People also like to listen to rock music from the United States and *tejano* (teh-HAHN-oh) music, which combines Mexican and American styles.

Mariachi (mah-ree-AH-chee) bands are well known. It is said these bands started during the French occupation of Mexico, when they played at weddings. The name comes from the French word *mariage* (marriage). During the revolution, mariachi became traveling musicians who played for tips. Today, there are mariachi bands all over Mexico, and even some in the United States and Canada.

Crafts

Popular art forms are everywhere in Mexico. Craft skills such as weaving, pottery-making, and silver work have been practiced for thousands of years. Silver work shows both Indian and Spanish influence. Colonial silver is usually very intricate, in a style called filigree, but modern silver is returning to simpler designs. Pottery and weaving have benefited enormously from tourism.

WOMEN'S CRAFTS

Can you imagine pulling a whole shawl through a ring? The *rebozos* (ree-BOH-sohs) that Mexican women weave are so fine that you can do exactly that. Many of the traditional crafts in Mexico, such as brightly colored ponchos, blankets, skirts, and pottery bowls and jars, are made by women. These traditions are passed on from mother to daughter.
(A Closer Look, page 72)

Below: A mariachi band usually includes three violins, a five- and a six-stringed guitar, a bass guitar, and two trumpets.

Left: This woman in colorful skirts is performing a ballet folklorico dance from the state of Jalisco. Each region of Mexico has its own style of dance and costumes. The most popular dance troupe is the Ballet Folklorico in Mexico City. They perform Spanish dances as well as Indian dances and music. For example, one of their dances, the "Yaqui Indian Stag Dance," is a traditional dance from northern Mexico. The troupe has performed all over the world and can be seen most weeks in the Institute of Fine Arts in Mexico City.

The Muralists

The three most important post-revolutionary artists were Diego Rivera, José Clemente Orozco, and David Siqueiros. All three used the mural tradition of the pre-Columbian Indians to show scenes from Mexican history. Siqueiros painted what is perhaps the world's largest mural painting, called *The March of Humanity on Earth and Towards the Cosmos*. It covers an area of 5,380 square yards (4,500 square m) and was painted single-handedly by him! He decorated both the inside and the outside of the Polyforum Cultural Siqueiros building in Mexico City. Orozco's greatest work is a mural in the Palacio de Gobierno (Government Palace) showing Father Hidalgo going to battle for Mexican independence from Spain. Diego Rivera's most well-known murals are at the National Palace in Mexico City.

PAINTERS OF THE REVOLUTION

The painters Diego Rivera and Frida Kahlo were both enthusiastic supporters of the Mexican Revolution and its ideals. Their passion for painting also drew them together, and they were married in 1929.

(A Closer Look, page 61)

Leisure and Festivals

Mexicans spend their leisure time much like everyone else in the modern world. Mexican television shows, especially soap operas, are very popular among adults and are even shown in other countries in South America. There is also a large film industry, with popular stars. People in the countryside often do not have television sets or movie theaters so they spend their time visiting with neighbors or planning the next fiesta.

Village fiestas, or festivals, are very important in Mexico, and people spend a long time preparing for them. Musicians and dancers practice, costumes are made, and money is saved to pay for the food and drinks. You could go to a fiesta almost every day of the year if you traveled around Mexico. Every village has a celebration for their patron saint as well as for national holidays. There are many religious holidays as well as secular, or nonreligious ones.

Below: **Mexico is said to celebrate more festivals than any other country in Latin America. These two children are colorfully dressed for a local fiesta.**

Left: **For special parties, children get a *piñata* (peen-YAH-tah) to play with. This is a clay pot filled with candies and covered with crepe paper. All the children are blindfolded and given a stick to try to break the pot. The adults raise and lower the piñata on a rope to make it more difficult. Finally, someone breaks the pot, and everyone gets candy.**

Children's Games

Mexican children, like children everywhere in the world, are very inventive in their games. Some popular children's games are "Maria Blanca" and "Juan Pirulero." In "Maria Blanca," (Mary White), one child is chosen to be Maria while the others hold hands and form a circle around her. Another child is "it" and has to try to break into the circle to capture Maria. Maria is allowed to leave the circle to escape "it" but has to get back in to be safe. If she's caught, she has to be "it" and someone else is chosen to be Maria. "Juan Pirulero" is very similar to "Simon Says." All the children except "Juan" choose to do a certain action with their hands, such as ironing, writing, or playing the guitar. Juan pretends to play the clarinet while singing a song. At any time, Juan can start imitating one of the other children. That child then has to play the clarinet and continue the song until Juan switches back again. Juan continues to switch activities back and forth until someone gets confused and does the wrong thing. Then he or she becomes Juan.

Fútbol and Baseball

The most popular sport in all of Latin America is *fútbol* (FOOT-bohl), or soccer. Everyone starts playing at an early age. Soccer has become a popular international game because it does not require much equipment. Most villages in Mexico, no matter how small, will have a soccer field and a ball. School teams from Mexico and Texas in the United States will also sometimes meet for games. The Azteca Stadium in Mexico City can seat a hundred thousand people, and games are held in the summer on Thursday evenings and Sunday afternoons.

In northern Mexico, along the U.S. border, baseball and American football are also becoming popular. Children play baseball in school as well as in baseball leagues. The Mexican League plays during the summer. Professional teams participate in the Caribbean World Series, which is held in Mexico every few years. One of the best teams is the Naranjeros from Hermosillo. They won the Caribbean World Series in 1976; the Mexicali won in 1986. Some of the best players are recruited by U.S. baseball teams, although there is always an outcry when this happens!

CHARROS: MEXICAN COWBOYS

Mexican rodeos are a national sport. Cowboys, or *charros* (CHAH-rohz), show off their skills riding horses, roping, and bull-riding.
(A Closer Look, page 48)

Below: Soccer, or *fútbol*, is a popular sport for adults and children alike.

Bullfighting

Bullfighting is a sport in Mexico that survives from the Spanish colonial period. It is one of the most popular spectator sports and draws huge crowds. The largest bullfighting ring in the world, the Plaza de Toros, is in Mexico City and seats fifty thousand people.

Bullfighting is considered an art form by many, rather than just a sport. It is a test of the matador's, or bullfighter's, skill and control over his or her own fear. The fight begins when a handkerchief is waved and the bull rushes into the ring. The matador must try to kill the bull by stabbing him with a sword between the shoulder blades. The matador waves a pink or red cape in front of the bull to make the bull charge. Several other men first weaken, but also anger, the bull by piercing him between the shoulder blades with spears and barbed sticks. The furious bull then charges. The matador has sixteen minutes to kill the bull, or else the fight is over.

Although the sport is often cruel, the bulls are not always killed. Sometimes the matador is seriously injured or even killed. And sometimes, the excited yet sympathetic crowds will cheer to save the courageous bull's life.

Above: **Bullfighting is a test of strength as well as control for the bullfighter. He or she uses a pink or red cape to provoke the bull into charging.**

Religious Festivals

On January 6, Mexicans celebrate the Epiphany, the day when the three kings visited Jesus in Bethlehem and brought him gifts of gold, frankincense, and myrrh. This, rather than December 25, is the traditional gift-giving day. Children leave their shoes outside their door, and in the morning, the shoes are filled with presents.

In Catholicism, the forty days before Easter are called Lent. This is a time when people must give up something they really like, to recreate the suffering of Jesus before he died. Since this is such a serious time, Catholics have a big party called Carnaval in February before Lent. There are parades, music, and dancing. People dress up in costumes inspired by Mexican history, such as those of the Spanish conquerors, or dress as soldiers or devils.

Easter in Mexico is more than just one day. The celebration often lasts a whole week, called Holy Week, in March or April. Mexicans visit their church at this time for special masses and prepare feasts to enjoy with their families.

DAY OF THE DEAD

This is a day when Mexicans remember their loved ones who have died. People may dress up as skeletons during processions or leave offerings of sugar skulls at the graves.

(*A Closer Look*, page 52)

Independence Day

This holiday, from September 15 to 16, commemorates the day that Father Hidalgo, a priest in the town of Dolores, started the Mexican War of Independence in 1810. He rallied the people of his village using the church bell, and his battle cry was, "Long live independence and death to the Spaniards!" This is called *El Grito de Dolores*, the Cry of Dolores. Independence Day is celebrated with a show of fireworks in Mexico City, and huge crowds gather in the main square. The president begins the celebrations by repeating Father Hidalgo's battle cry from the balcony of the presidential palace. He then rings a replica of Father Hidalgo's bell. This scene is recreated in every town in Mexico, with the mayor reciting the battle cry and ringing a bell.

Cinco de Mayo

On May 5, Mexicans commemorate the 1862 Battle of Puebla when Benito Juárez and his army first beat the French troops who were attempting to take over Mexico.

Birthday of Benito Juárez

Benito Juárez was the first Indian president of Mexico. There is an official holiday on his birthday, March 21.

Opposite: **Easter is an important holiday in Mexico. People take part in processions, and one tradition is to burn a large model of Judas, the person who betrayed Christ.**

Food

Modern Mexican food is a blend of native Indian, Spanish, French, and recently, American food. The traditional staple is corn, which is eaten with beans and squash. Before the Spaniards arrived, Mexicans did not eat food cooked in oil or fat, and their only animal meat was from dogs and occasionally wild turkeys and ducks.

Corn and Beans

Corn tortillas are the basis of many meals. They are used in a variety of dishes including *tacos* (TAH-kohs), which are tortillas with meat, *enchiladas* (en-chee-LAH-dahs), which are soft tortillas filled and covered with chili sauce, *quesadillas* (kay-sah-DEE-as), filled with cheese and fried, and *panuchos* (pan-OO-chos), stuffed with beans and fried. Corn meal is also used to make *tamales* (tah-MAH-lays), which are a combination of corn and meat wrapped in a corn husk and steamed. Another traditional food, still very popular, is beans. The most common way to eat beans in Mexico is as *frijoles refritos* (free-HOH-lays re-FREE-tohs), refried, boiled, brown kidney beans.

TOMATOES, ANYONE?

Tomatoes were unknown to the rest of the world until the Spaniards went to Mexico. Potatoes, avocados, corn, and chilies also came from the Americas. Can you imagine food today without these ingredients?
(*A Closer Look, page 66*)

Below: **Corn tortillas are being cooked on a large, hot griddle for passersby in this street market.**

Above: **These colorful drinks are known as *aguas frescas* (AH-gwas FRES-kahs). They are sold from large jars on the streets in cities, and are made from fruit and grain boiled together, strained, then chilled with ice.**

Drinks

Mexicans drink a lot of coffee, usually with plenty of sugar and milk. Hot chocolate originated in Mexico and was a drink primarily for royalty. Today, many people add cinnamon to their hot chocolate. *Pulque* (POOL-kay) is a traditional alcoholic drink made from the pulp of agave. It was the only alcoholic drink before the Spaniards arrived. The Spaniards invented another famous Mexican alcohol called *mescal* (MAYS-kahl) by fermenting the pulp of agave. Other popular drinks today include *jugos* (HOO-gohs), which are fresh fruit or vegetable juices, *licuados* (lee-KWA-dohs), which are juices combined with either water or milk, and *limonada* (lee-mohn-AH-dah), or fresh lemonade. These drinks can be purchased from market vendors.

Mealtimes

Most Mexicans eat a very light breakfast of coffee and sweet breads. Their main meal of the day, *comida* (koh-MEE-dah), is eaten around 2 o'clock in the afternoon. It includes a soup, a main course, and a dessert. The whole family eats together whenever possible. People usually have a siesta, or rest, afterward.

CHOCOLATE: THE DRINK OF THE GODS!

Chocolate first came to us from the Aztecs! It was a special drink for the king of the Aztecs, Montezuma, and was taken back to Spain by Hernán Cortés.

(A Closer Look, page 50)

A CLOSER LOOK AT MEXICO

Did you know that chocolate comes from Mexico? If you are surprised, read on to find how many foods you eat originally came from Mexico. Other Mexican foods, such as cactus leaves and fruit, may seem rather unusual.

This section also elaborates on Mexico's unique culture and interesting history. The Aztec Indians had a mighty empire before their conquest by the Spanish. Aztec influence continues to this day in religion, art, and the language. Their celebrations are part of modern-day festivals, such as the Day of the Dead and the Feast of the Virgin of Guadalupe. Although most people converted to Catholicism under Spanish rule, many Indians combined this new religion with their old gods. When sick or in trouble, they do not hesitate to call on either.

After reading this section, you will know all about Mexico's cowboys and the exciting test of their skills during a rodeo. Beautiful crafts by women have become popular worldwide. You will also be able to talk about the religion, art, and writers of Mexico like an expert!

Above: **These young people have learned how to dance ballet folklorico. Their shoes have taps made out of many nails and contribute to great rhythms as they stamp their feet to the music. Both adults and children may perform at large festivals.**

Opposite: **Young Indian girls from the state of Chiapas, in southern Mexico.**

The Aztecs

Nomadic Warriors

The Indian tribe known as the Aztecs was originally called the Mexica. Does the name sound familiar? Mexico, Mexico City, and New Mexico were named after the Mexica. The Mexica, or Aztecs, were nomads, meaning they did not live in one place, but traveled around. They made their living by raiding settled farming communities and cities, and were known to be cruel and quarrelsome. Yet they were also known to be extremely brave and did not seem to fear death. This enabled the Aztecs to conquer the settled peoples of the Valley of Mexico and beyond.

An Eagle Eating a Snake

The Aztecs believed in a sun god named Huitzilopochtli. He was a very demanding god who, according to their legends, decided what the Aztecs should do and who they should fight. Huitzilopochtli told the people to settle in a place where they saw an eagle sitting on a cactus eating a snake.

Above: **The Aztec emblem of an eagle holding a snake and sitting on a cactus is still the Mexican crest and also appears on the Mexican flag.**

Below: **This mural by Diego Rivera shows Montezuma, the Aztec king, seated in the middle. There is a busy marketplace in front of him. In the background, one can see the lake waters around which the city was built.**

The Aztecs found their eagle on a small island in the middle of a lake and established their capital, Tenochtitlán, in 1325. After the Spanish conquest, this became Mexico City.

The Aztec Empire

Over the next hundred years, the Aztecs established a productive city based on a type of farming called *chinampas* (chee-NAHM-pahs). Because their city was surrounded by water, they had no dry land to farm. They designed a creative system of gardens, where food was grown on rafts floating in the lake. The Aztecs were not a peaceful people and soon started fighting with their neighbors. As they conquered more and more neighboring cities, they became stronger and stronger. By the time the Spaniards arrived in 1519, the Mexica, or Aztecs as they came to be known, controlled most of the Valley of Mexico and demanded tribute from many groups. It was because they demanded so much tribute and killed so many people for their god, that many of the other Indian groups were unhappy under Aztec control. These Indians became allies with the Spaniards and helped defeat the powerful Aztec empire.

Above: **This strange wall of skulls is from the main Aztec temple, Templo Mayor. It was dedicated to the gods of war and rain, and the skulls are believed to belong to victims who were sacrificed.**

AZTEC SOCIETY

Aztec society was very complex, with three classes of people: nobles, commoners, and slaves. Slaves were people captured in wars and sometimes killed in religious rituals for Huitzilopochtli, the sun god.

Cactus and Century Plants

There are many different species of cacti and other succulents in Mexico. More than one hundred and twenty species of cacti occur in Baja California alone. With this diversity, it is not surprising that people have learned to put some to use. Several types are eaten, while others are used by Indians as hallucinogens. Prickly pear is one kind of cactus that can be eaten. Certain agaves, or century plants, can be tapped to make alcohol.

Left: A stack of cactus for sale in a Mexico City market. The large, flattened stems of some species of prickly pear cactus do not have spines, and the plants are widely grown for food and forage for cattle. They are also known as Indian figs.

Prickly Pears

Prickly pear cactus, or *nopal* (no-PAHL), is native to North and South America and is cultivated in Mexico for a variety of uses. Its reddish fruit, the prickly pear, is edible. The fruit is eaten raw in salads or made into marmalade. It is a good source of vegetable fat and protein. The flowers of the cactus are used to make a tea, which is believed to bring down fevers. The stems of spineless varieties are also eaten by people. Water is stored by the cactus in its flat, fleshy stems — sometimes these are fed to livestock as a source of liquid if nothing else is available in a drought.

Agave

The agave, or century plant, is also cultivated in Mexico. There are different varieties of agave — one of them produces a sweet sap. When this sap is fermented, it produces the drink known as *pulque* (POOL-kay), which is mildly alcoholic. Before the Spaniards came, only older people in the Aztec empire were allowed to drink pulque. The Spaniards introduced the technique of distilling pulque into a purer alcohol. This purer form is called *tequila* (tay-KEE-lah) after the town where it was first made.

Top and *above:* The mature fruit of the agave, or century plant, is collected for its sap known as "honey water." Alcoholic drinks can be made from the sap — fermented for pulque or distilled for tequila.

Charros: Mexican Cowboys

Cattle Ranching Skills

Mexico has its own cowboys, called *charros* (CHAR-rohz). A charro must have many skills — roping, tying cattle, and riding horses. The charros originated early on in colonial history, when the Spaniards first started grazing cattle in Mexico. To brand the

Left: Charros take great pride in their costumes and have several different types. For work or competition, they wear simple, sturdy pants, boots, and shirts. Their fancier costume includes tight pants, a white shirt and a wide-brimmed hat, along with a short jacket and bow tie. Jackets and pants are fastened with buttons made of gold or silver, the hat is often embroidered with silver thread, and the pistol may be decorated.

animals or collect some for meat or hides, men had to ride out on horseback and use their skills of roping, steer wrangling, and herding. These men became known as charros. One of the techniques they used to separate cows from the herd was called *rodeo* (roh-DAY-oh), which in Spanish means "round." A group of men on horseback would form a circle around a group of cattle to separate them from the herd and move them away. This is the origin of the English word rodeo, meaning a contest of cattle-ranching skills.

During the nineteenth century, charros fought in the war for Mexican independence. They also fought against the French invaders, and later, they fought the Americans in the Mexican–American War. They added the pistol and gunbelt to their normal costume to represent their tradition of fighting for Mexico's rights and freedom.

Competing in a Charreada

To show off their skills today, charros participate in rodeos, or *charreadas* (chah-ray-AH-dahs). In ranching regions of Mexico, some towns host charreadas every month of the year in special arenas called charro rings. A charreada is similar to a rodeo in the American West. The charro first demonstrates his skill in riding a horse. He also shows off his skills with a rope, forming large, spinning, lasso circles in the air. He must also successfully ride a bull and grab a wild bull by the tail and roll it over on its back.

Above: **Competing in a charreada includes riding horses and showing off one's skill with lassos. There are strict rules of conduct, and the competitors work very hard at perfecting their skills, designing their dress costumes, and acquiring equipment for their horses.**

Chocolate: the Drink of the Gods!

A Drink for Aztec Royalty

Chocolate is made from cacao beans, which grow on a tree called the cacao tree. The Latin name for this tree is *Theobroma cacao*. Theobroma means "drink of the gods." You might think it is a little bit strange to call chocolate a "drink," but originally, this is how people consumed chocolate.

The story of chocolate is fascinating — this is what happened: When the Spanish conqueror Hernán Cortés first came to Mexico in 1519, he met Montezuma, king of the Aztecs. He saw Montezuma drinking a spicy cocoa liquid from golden cups. This drink was considered very special because the beans that produced cocoa were also exchanged as money by the Aztecs. It was as if the king was drinking money! Cortés tasted the drink but found it very bitter. However, he decided to bring some cacao beans back to Spain so the Spaniards could grow cacao trees and have Aztec money for trade. "Money" plantations were started on some of the Caribbean islands. People in Spain also decided to change the bitter, spicy recipe of Montezuma by adding hot water and sugar to ground-up cacao beans. This was the first sweet hot chocolate!

Above: **Chocolate is loved all over the world now, but it came originally from Mexico.**

The First Chocolate Bar

The drink became more and more popular in Europe, and by the 1700s, you could go to a chocolate house in London instead of a coffee house. Chocolate became affordable for poor people when machines were designed to process the cocoa beans faster. It was not until 1828 that a Dutch chemist learned how to press the cocoa to remove some of the fat, called cocoa butter. Soon someone discovered that extra cocoa butter and sugar could be added to ground cacao beans, and the first chocolate bar was made!

Today, cacao trees are grown on plantations in Mexico, Central America, the Caribbean Islands, and West Africa. The seeds are taken out of the pods and dried for a few days. They are cleaned, roasted, and shelled. The inside of the seed, called the nib, is pressed in large machines to remove the chocolate liquor or juice. This is the product from which all chocolate products are made. If the liquor is pressed again, cocoa butter is extracted, leaving cocoa powder. To make chocolate candy, extra cocoa butter is added to chocolate liquor and of course, sugar, since unsweetened cocoa is very bitter. White chocolate is made by using just cocoa butter.

Today, chocolate is no longer only for kings. Everyone can enjoy it as a drink, as candy, or as a flavor for ice cream, but we owe it all to a Mexican king named Montezuma!

Left: Cacao beans grow in pods that hang off the trunk and branches of the tree. When the pods are ripe, they usually change color to become red, purple, or dark green.

SPICY CHOCOLATE?

Mexicans use chocolate in a spicy sauce for meat dishes such as chicken. This sauce is called *mole* (MOH-lay) and combines onion, garlic, chilies, sesame or pumpkin seeds, and Mexican chocolate to make a rich, dark sauce. This is a traditional dish that dates back to Aztec times.

Day of the Dead

Remembering the Dead

The Day of the Dead, or Día de los Muertos, on November 1 and 2, is one of the largest festivals in Mexico. It is a time for remembering loved ones who have died. The festival is a mixture of the Catholic celebration of All Saints' Day and ancient Aztec beliefs. The Aztecs used to remember the dead for two whole months every year, one month for children and one month for adults. Today, the festival lasts only for one day and two nights, but some Aztec symbolism is still used. For example, Aztecs thought yellow flowers were sacred to their dead. Today, many people clean the graves of family members and put marigold flowers on their graves. They also place flowers on the path leading to the family altar. Fresh flowers and offerings of food are laid at roadside shrines throughout the country. Mexicans, like the ancient Aztecs, believe that the dead return to the world of the living on these days to rejoice and celebrate with them. This is not a sad day, but a happy one with everyone reunited.

Below: Families visit the cemeteries at night, lighting candles, offering food, and placing pictures of saints or wreaths of flowers at the graves of their loved ones. They may stay all night telling stories about the people who have died.

Left: Calaveras are sugar skulls made for the Day of the Dead. They are offered at the grave for returning souls. Mexicans believe the dead love sweet things and bread more than anything else.

Skulls, Skeletons, and Other Candy

Preparations for this festival begin a long time in advance. Special treats and food are made for both the living and the dead. Two kinds of food are traditional at this time: *calaveras* (kah-lah-VAY-rahs) and *pan de muerto* (PAN DAY moo-EHR-toh), bread of the dead. Calaveras are candies in the shape of skulls and skeletons, made from sugar and decorated in bright colors. Bread of the dead is also sweet, and often there is a toy skeleton hidden inside. It is considered good luck if you are the one to bite into the skeleton. Special dishes, such as meat with spicy sauces and other favorite foods of the dead person, are also made for this day.

Families bring food for a picnic near the grave and sometimes stay through the night in the cemetery, eating and drinking with the souls of their dead family members. There are two days for celebration because November 1 is thought to be the day when the souls of dead children return, and November 2 is for adults.

NO TIME FOR SORROW

Surprisingly, people do not get sad remembering the dead. They say the path back to the living must not be made slippery with tears, meaning the dead do not want the living to cry and be sad. They want to come back and enjoy their favorite foods and drinks.

Magic in Mexico

Offerings to the Gods

In isolated rural communities, people still believe in their traditional gods and the rituals they practiced before Christianity became the main religion. Mexico's Indians have been Christian for a long time, but they combine old and new customs to form their own type of belief system. For example, during planting and harvesting, many Indians still make offerings to the old gods and goddesses. In some areas, they do this by "planting" bread and chocolate in the ground to ask the rain god for good weather for

Left: **This woman is part of celebrations for the Virgin of Guadalupe feast. She is making an offering to the Aztec sun god by burning copal, a type of tree resin. Although it is a Christian celebration, there are many Aztec elements in the festivities.**

their crops. In other areas, people sacrifice roosters to ask for fertility in the fields. Stone images of Indian gods are hidden in the countryside. People make offerings of food to these images in times of need to ask for rain or good luck.

Curanderos

Health care is a part of Mexican life that clearly shows the combination of old and new beliefs. Rural villages may not always have a nurse or doctor, but they will usually have a *curandero* (koor-ahn-DAY-roh), or healer. Curanderos are men or women who have learned how to treat an illness with special herbs and foods. Some of the diseases they treat are not recognized by doctors. For example, many Mexican Indians believe in *mal ojo* (MAL OH-hoh), which means the "evil eye." The belief is that some people can cause harm to others by giving them the evil eye. If you get the evil eye, you can become very sick and only the curandero can help.

The curandero may use special herbs combined with common foods, such as eggs or oil, to cure a person. He or she may appeal to Catholic saints at the same time — the two belief systems may go hand in hand. The curandero also tries to work with the whole community, and if there is a conflict within families or between neighbors, may ask other people to participate in the healing of the sick person to relieve any social stress.

Mexico City

With about sixteen million inhabitants, Mexico City is one of the largest cities in the world. It is located in the Valley of Mexico at 7,000 feet (2,100 m) above sea level. The city is surrounded by volcanic mountains, some of which, such as Mt. Popocatépetl, are still active. The area is also subject to earthquakes, and the last one in 1985 killed ten thousand people. Because there are so many people, Mexico City faces some difficult urban problems — polluted air and a shortage of water. Air pollution is very severe because the city is in a natural bowl formed by the mountains, and pollution from cars and industry cannot blow away. Despite the hazards, Mexico City is a vibrant place, the cultural capital of Mexico, and draws many people every year looking for jobs.

The Aztec Capital

Mexico city was founded on the same site as the Aztec capital, Tenochtitlán. When the Spaniards first arrived in 1519, Tenochtitlán was a large urban center of three hundred thousand people living on reclaimed land in the middle of a lake. Long stone bridges connected the city with the shore. When Hernán Cortés took over the city, he tore down all the Aztec buildings. Over time, the lake dried up as the city expanded.

Below: Mexico City has some of the worst air pollution in the world. Factories that surround the city pump high amounts of sulfur dioxide into the air. Cars in the city also contribute to the problem, and there are restrictions now on the number of cars allowed on the road at any one time.

Above: **A bustling street market in Mexico City.**

Sinking and No Water

Although the original lake waters have disappeared from the surface, there are still large reserves of water underground. The first layer of soil is clay, and underneath is sand. As Mexico City grew, wells were sunk into the sand to extract water. Eventually, as more and more water was drawn up for the city's needs, rain runoff from the surrounding mountains could not replace the underground water fast enough. The water level has decreased to the point that the clay soils are no longer water-soaked. As a result, the clay is now unstable and sinks into the sandy parts underneath. In older parts of the city, you can see buildings that have tilted to one side or are sinking lower than the nearby streets. Some of the important historic buildings, such as the National Cathedral, have steel supports, but many other buildings just continue to sink and tilt.

There are now too many people in Mexico City and not enough water. As many as two million new arrivals to the city live in slums with no running water and no sewers. Other people have to depend on water trucks to bring their water. Mexico City presents a difficult challenge to urban planners.

Mexico's Famous Writers

Mexico has a very rich literary tradition. Many Mexican writers are recognized worldwide, and their books are regularly published in English. Five of the best known outside Mexico are Carlos Fuentes, Octavio Paz, Elena Poniatowska, María Luisa Puga, and Laura Esquivel.

Octavio Paz was awarded the Nobel Prize for Literature in 1990. He is a poet and essayist and is also known for his political commitment to social justice. He published his first work of poetry, *Luna Silvestre,* in 1933, when he was nineteen. His best known work is an essay about Mexican identity called "The Labyrinth of Solitude" (1950). He also served as a diplomat for Mexico in India (1962–1968) but resigned in protest over Mexico's treatment of student radicals. He lived and taught in universities in the United States and Europe for many years.

Below, left: Octavio Paz, born in 1914, is a well-known Mexican poet, writer, and diplomat.

Below, right: Carlos Fuentes has also had a career in both writing and diplomacy.

Carlos Fuentes was born in 1928 in Mexico City. His varied career has included writing novels, short stories, and plays, work as a critic, and serving as a diplomat for Mexico. His father was also a diplomat, and Fuentes traveled through much of North and South America and Europe as a child with his family. He went on to study law at the National University of Mexico and attended the Institute of Advanced International Studies in Geneva. He had a successful career as a diplomat, representing Mexico at the United Nations and in France, where he served as ambassador from 1975 to 1977.

Above: **Laura Esquivel's novel,** *Como Agua Para Chocolate (Like Water for Chocolate),* **has been translated into English and turned into a movie.**

Fuentes became a communist in the 1950s but left the party in 1962, although continuing to believe in Marxism. His first collection of stories was written in 1954, and his first novel, *Where the Air is Clear*, was written in 1958. His writing was experimental, and he became famous for new techniques that included influences from non-Spanish literature. He continued to travel widely, as he had in his youth. *The Death of Artemio Cruz* (1962), about the Mexican Revolution, is Fuentes's most famous book. It was translated into several European languages as well as English and established Fuentes's international reputation. He has won literary prizes in Mexico, Spain, and Venezuela for his writing.

Elena Poniatowska is a novelist and journalist. Her first job was for a newspaper in 1954, and soon she became known for her excellent skills as an interviewer. Her most famous book is called *Massacre in Mexico* (1975) about the clash between students and the army in 1968, which left many young people dead. She has also written about the earthquake in Mexico City in 1985 and the life of a woman who fought in the Mexican Revolution.

Maria Luisa Puga writes novels, short stories, and essays. Her most famous novel is *The Possibilities of Hate* about racism in Kenyan society. Her books and stories are usually about the problems of gender and racial differences in Mexican society.

Laura Esquivel is the newest addition to the list of famous Mexican writers. Her first novel, *Like Water for Chocolate* (1989), became an instant bestseller in Mexico and has been published in English. The movie (1992) based on the novel was very popular in the United States and Canada and won awards in Mexico.

Painters of the Revolution

Diego Rivera and Frida Kahlo are two of Mexico's most famous artists. They were married to each other in 1929, and some of Kahlo's work reflects her relationship with Rivera. Both artists were supporters of the Mexican Revolution and were part of a group of left-wing intellectuals in Mexico.

Frida Kahlo (1907–1954)

Frida Kahlo was born in 1907. She did not start to paint until a bad traffic accident in 1925 left her with a fractured spine. She started to teach herself to paint, and Diego Rivera, whom she married in 1929, encouraged her in her work.

Many of Kahlo's paintings are self-portraits in which she shows herself in native Indian dress. Her art was part of a cultural revival of the Indian part of Mexico's heritage. Unlike her husband, Kahlo was not given international recognition for her work until after her death. She is now seen as one of the twentieth century's great woman painters.

Diego Rivera (1886–1957)

Diego Rivera is best known for his many murals, or wall paintings. He studied art in Mexico, then spent ten years in Paris, from 1911 to 1921, planning a form of popular art that could reflect the new society created by the Mexican Revolution. His work was strongly rooted in Mexican traditions and resulted in a revival of wall painting.

Many of Rivera's murals can be seen in and around Mexico City. One of his most ambitious projects was the series of murals on the main courtyard and staircase of the National Palace in Mexico City. These paintings show Mexican history, from the golden age of pre-conquest Indian society to the Spanish conquest, war, independence, and the Revolution of 1910. Father Hidalgo, Benito Juárez, Emiliano Zapata, and "Pancho" Villa are all among the historical figures painted by Rivera. He was also commissioned to paint murals in the United States, but much of his work was thought too radical and controversial.

Above: **A statue of the artist Frida Kahlo. She was badly traumatized by a streetcar accident and turned to painting. Proud, yet deeply tormented inside, her agony is reflected in many self-portraits.**

Opposite: **This is one of Diego Rivera's murals at the National Palace. It shows scenes from life in Mexico prior to the conquest by Spain. The central figure is a high-ranking Huastec Indian, wearing quetzal feathers in his hair. There are typical pyramid-shaped temples in the background, and men dressed as birds swing from a pole in the center as part of an ancient ceremony.**

The Spanish Conquest

Hernán Cortés Lands in Mexico

Until 1519, the Aztec empire knew nothing of Europeans. But within two years, this mighty state was conquered, and all its people forced to obey the laws of Spain. The amazing part of this story is that the conquest was largely the work of one man, Hernán Cortés, who had only a few soldiers and horses.

Cortés was sent by the Spanish governor of Cuba, Diego Velázquez, to explore the coast of Mexico. He was thirty-four years old and anxious to make his fortune. He landed near Veracruz on Good Friday in 1519 and was soon greeted by messengers sent by the Aztec king, Montezuma. They brought gifts of gold necklaces, beautifully colored textiles, a turquoise mask, and huge disks of hammered gold and silver. Cortés decided to investigate the source of this treasure.

Word of the strange white men with horses had quickly reached Montezuma, who decided that Cortés might be an Aztec god named Quetzalcoatl. Aztec legend said Quetzalcoatl would come from the east — the same direction Cortés took. The Aztecs had also never seen horses and believed them to be a special kind of giant deer that could hunt down enemies.

MALINALI

Cortés would not have been as successful as he was if he did not have the help of an Indian woman named Malinali. She could speak the two most important Indian languages, Nahuatl, of the Aztecs, and Maya. Malinali also knew a lot about the Aztecs and how their society worked. Her work as interpreter made it possible for Cortés to get the help of Indian groups who did not like the Aztecs.

Tecoaccinco.

Left: **Hernán Cortés receiving presents from the Indians.**

Cortés sent some of Montezuma's gifts back to Spain with a letter explaining that he had decided to settle the new land in the name of Charles I, the king of Spain. To prevent his men from leaving, he had all the ships destroyed on the beach. Totonac Indians, who were unhappy with the Aztecs, became allies of Cortés. With several hundred of his own men and four hundred Indian warriors of the Totonac tribe, Cortés headed inland to find and conquer the Aztec capital, Tenochtitlán. Along the way, he met many other Indian groups, some of which joined him. Without these Indian allies, Cortés might never have succeeded.

Above: **One of the Indian groups that Cortés encountered, the Tlaxcalans, fought bravely against the Spanish weapons at first. But eventually they made peace since neither side could win. The Tlaxcalans had resisted the Aztec warriors for years and decided to help Cortés defeat them once and for all.**

The Defeat of Montezuma, the Aztec King

After a long and tiring journey, Cortés reached Tenochtitlán on November 8, 1519. Montezuma came out to greet him, and the two exchanged gifts. But Cortés soon had the Aztec king imprisoned, and six months later he returned to Tenochtitlán with a larger army sent by the governor of Cuba. He laid siege to the city and finally captured it on August 13, 1521, just two years after he first arrived.

Taxco: Town of Silver

Taxco became part of the Aztec empire in the mid-1400s. As in other places under their control, the Aztecs made the local people pay a tax to the king. The people of Taxco paid their taxes in copper. When Cortés arrived in Mexico in 1519, he heard a rumor that Taxco paid its taxes in pure gold, and he sent his men to investigate. They found no gold but did find tin and iron in the

Left: **José de la Borda felt so blessed by God he decided to build a church in Taxco in thanks. The church he built is called Santa Prisca and is still one of the most beautiful churches in Mexico. The clock of Santa Prisca was designed by Isaac Rogers, the same man who designed Big Ben in London, England.**

Left: Taxco is still a center for skilled silversmiths, some of whose families have worked as silver artisans for many generations. Along with silver jewelry, one can buy a large assortment of silver items in Taxco, including candlesticks, vases, and bowls.

mines. By the 1530s, silver had also been discovered. Indians, under the control of the Spanish, were made to work in the mines like slaves, and all the metal was shipped back to Spain.

In 1716, José de la Borda came from Spain to join his brother working in the mines. The legend goes that on his way along the rocky mountain trail to Taxco, his horse stumbled on a rock that was almost pure silver. He and his brother founded one of the richest family mines in Mexican history.

Silver Jewelry

During the 1800s, very little silver was mined in Taxco due to low prices and the distance from Mexico City. But in the 1920s, silver mining received a new burst of energy when William Spratling, an American, started making silver jewelry in Taxco. He based his designs on the art of Mexico's ancient Indian cultures. He was also the first person to combine native materials, such as onyx, with silver. He trained local Mexicans at his workshop and attracted other Americans to start their own workshops. During World War II, Americans could not get any silver from Europe so they started buying from Taxco. This inspired many more workshops to open. In the 1960s, many Mexican silversmiths stopped using ancient designs and turned to more modern styles of jewelry.

Tomatoes, Anyone?

When you think of Mexican food, you probably imagine tacos, burritos, enchiladas, and quesadillas, which are all definitely Mexican. What you may not realize is there are many other foods we eat everyday that were discovered and cooked by Mexican Indians long before the arrival of Europeans. These foods have become so much a part of our diet, we no longer remember them as particularly Mexican in origin.

Before the Spanish conqueror Hernán Cortés came to Mexico, no one in Europe had ever seen a tomato! This plant is native to Mesoamerica (Middle America, including Mexico and Central America). After his conquest, plants were taken back to Europe where they grew quite well and were combined with European foods. Imagine Italian food without tomatoes!

Turkeys were also introduced to Europe from Mesoamerica. This was one of the few meats eaten before the Spaniards introduced cows, pigs, and sheep. The Aztec kings feasted on

Below: **Tomatoes, chilies, corn chips, and tortillas — all these foods came to other countries from Mexico originally. How many dishes do you eat with tomatoes in them? Ketchup, spaghetti sauce, pizza, and salads are only a few.**

Above: **Red peppers are spread outside to dry in the sun.**

turkey long before the first Thanksgiving dinner was ever cooked! Corn and beans are also native to the Americas. The Aztecs showed the Spanish how to process and cook the corn to make breads and pancakes. Since then, corn has been carefully bred to change its color and taste, but the original plants were American, not European. We now eat corn as a fresh vegetable, in corn flour and even in sweet corn syrup. The *aguacate* (ag-wah-KAH-tay), or avocado, was also brought to Europe by Cortés. The most popular way to eat it is still the Mexican dish called *guacamole* (gwa-kah-MO-lay), which is mashed avocado with onion, tomato, chilies, and cilantro.

In the United States, you can also eat food known as Tex-Mex, which is a combination of cooking styles from central Mexico and Texas. If you want to try an authentic Mexican dish, you should try chicken with *mole* (MOH-lay) sauce. Mole is either brown or green and is made from unsweetened chocolate, spices, and chilies. If you like that, you may want to try the Mexican national dish, *chiles en nogada* (CHEE-lays en noh-GAH-dah), which combines Aztec and European elements. It is breaded peppers stuffed with meat and pine nuts (Aztec) covered with a sweet, walnut cream sauce (Spanish) and garnished with parsley and pomegranate seeds.

Buen Provecho: "Enjoy your Meal!"

The Virgin of Guadalupe

Just outside Mexico City lies the town of Guadalupe. It is home to a famous church called the Basilica of Guadalupe, which houses a miraculous image of the Virgin Mary. Every year, millions of pilgrims come to pray. This is the story of how the image got there.

Left: During the Feast of the Virgin of Guadalupe, a large banner with the Virgin's image is hung outside the church. She is an important symbol for all Mexicans, Spanish and Indian. Early Spanish priests, who were trying to convince Indians to become Christian, showed the Indian Virgin (see next page) as an example to Indians that God cared about them too.

QUEEN OF MEXICO

While under Spanish rule, people in Mexico saw the Virgin as their special sign that Mexico was important to God. When there was an epidemic between 1736 and 1737 that killed many people, everyone prayed to the Virgin. They believed she stopped the epidemic. In 1910, the Virgin was made the patroness of all of Latin America. In 1945, Pope Pius XII called her the Empress of Latin America and the Queen of Mexico!

The Story of Juan Diego

In 1531, more than four hundred years ago, there was a poor Indian named Juan Diego. As the story goes, on his way to church one day, a lovely Indian lady appeared before him. She told Juan Diego that she was the Virgin Mary and asked him to go to the Bishop of Mexico, Juan de Zumárraga, to tell him to build a church in her honor. The bishop did not believe Juan at first and asked for a sign that the story was true. The next day the Virgin appeared to Juan Diego again and told him to gather roses from a certain place and take them to the bishop. Roses had never been seen there before but Juan found some. He gathered up the roses in his cape. When he opened the cape in front of the bishop, instead of roses, there was an image of the Virgin on the cape! The bishop was convinced, and a church was built for the Virgin Mary. Juan Diego's cape is still kept in the rebuilt church in Guadalupe.

The Virgin Mary is famous all over Mexico because she appeared to Juan Diego as an Indian woman. People throughout Latin America began to worship her, and in 1754, the pope gave her a special feast day, December 12. Many years later, when Mexico was fighting for independence from Spain, the Virgin of Guadalupe was its symbol of identity and a unifying force. Father Hidalgo used a picture of the Virgin on his banners as he led people to war with the Spaniards in 1810.

Above: **Every year in December, millions of people make a pilgrimage to Guadalupe to thank the Virgin Mary for answering their prayers. There is a big fiesta with food, dancing, and music. The *conchero* (kon-CHAY-roh) dancers perform in the large plaza outside the church. They wear Aztec clothing of feather headdresses and *conchas* (KON-chahs), or shells, around their ankles that add to the rhythm as they dance.**

¡Viva Zapata!

On January 1, 1994, a group of Indian peasants in the state of Chiapas started a rebellion. They named themselves *Zapatistas* (zah-pah-TEES-tahs) after one of the peasant heroes, Emiliano Zapata, of the Mexican Revolution in 1910. He is a legend among Mexico's Indians because he fought for their rights.

Who Was Emiliano Zapata?

Emiliano Zapata was born in a village in the state of Morelos in 1879. He was the ninth of ten children born to a very poor family. He learned to read and write, although he could not afford to finish primary school. At the time, around the turn of the twentieth century, many large land owners had taken away land from poor Indian farmers and made them work for very little money. Zapata helped farmers in his village defend their land in

Left: **Emiliano Zapata formed alliances with other rebels, including "Pancho" Villa in the northern state of Chihuahua, who was fighting for the same things. Zapata has become a legendary figure for Mexico's rural poor, and some believe he is still alive, hiding in the mountains and waiting for another chance to help them.**

the courts, and by 1909, he was elected president of the village council. He joined a revolution against Mexico's dictator, Porfirio Díaz, in 1910 and outlined the goals of the Indian rebels. These were: the return of land stolen by large landowners, the sharing of one-third of large farms among poor people who had no land, the rule of law, and democratic politics in the countryside. Many of these goals were later made law in the revolutionary constitution of 1917. He never saw the end of the revolution, however, because he was tricked by another general, trapped, and killed in 1919.

The Zapatistas in Chiapas

The 1994 rebels in Chiapas, although fighting eighty-four years later, called themselves Zapatistas because they wanted the same things Zapata fought for. They blockaded roads in Chiapas and seized land that belonged to large landowners. The government quickly stopped the rebellion and has tried to negotiate a peace settlement, admitting that the poor people of Chiapas need more land and money to survive. However, violence has continued to simmer between the Indians and local landowners and party officials, and in December 1997, forty-five unarmed Tzotzil Indians were killed in a massacre by paramilitaries.

Above: **"The land belongs to those who work on it," reads the banner at a Zapatista rally. The peasants are basically demanding a fairer distribution of land, as earlier promised in the constitution of 1917, based on Zapata's goals.**

LORD OF THE MOUNTAIN

The leader of the Zapatista rebels is called Subcommandante Marcos, but no one is certain who he is because he always wears a ski mask to hide his identity. He calls himself "owner of the night, lord of the mountain, man without a face, and with no tomorrow."

71

Women's Crafts

From remote mountain towns to shops throughout the world, the crafts of Mexico are evidence of the creativity and hard work of Indian women. These artisans follow traditional techniques learned from their mothers and grandmothers.

Beautiful Pottery

Both ancient and modern Indian cultures are well known for their beautiful pottery. They use an old technique called coiling. Instead of using a potter's wheel, Mexican potters roll the clay into long pieces, then coil them round and round to make the shape they want. Traditionally, it has been the woman's job to collect the clay from deposits in the countryside, shape the pots, and paint them with beautiful designs. Men help by collecting the wood used to fire the pots. A married woman has to know how to make many different pots including water jars, food storage jars, bowls, and plates. Girls may learn these skills at the young age of eleven.

Below: **Pots once made for everyday local use are now also made for sale all over the world.**

Woven Ponchos, Blankets, and Skirts

Mexican textiles come in many shapes and forms including wool blankets and ponchos, cotton shirts, skirts, and wall-hangings. Traditionally, women process the fibers, whether cotton or wool, and dye them using natural vegetable dyes. Each village or ethnic group has its own unique patterns woven or embroidered on the clothes. The traditional loom for weaving is called a backstrap loom because the weaver maintains tension in the threads with a strap wrapped around her body. This type of loom limits the width of the material to the width of a person. To make larger pieces of cloth, individual strips are sewn together.

Money for the Family

The crafts made by women are becoming more and more important to the family income because over the last twenty years, small family farmers have had a difficult time making ends meet. With the growth in tourism, many rural families now depend on the sale of these women's crafts to get much needed cash. Some families earn up to half or more of their income from the work of women. In some areas, women make more money by weaving than men do farming. This has brought some different problems for families, however, since it is the men who have traditionally been the breadwinners.

Above: **This woman is using a backstrap loom. The loom is stretched out to a tree or post in front of her and then strapped around her back and waist to maintain tension in the threads.**

RELATIONS WITH NORTH AMERICA

Mexico, Canada, and the United States are part of an important trade agreement called NAFTA. Although Mexico and the United States were at war with each other one hundred and fifty years ago, today, the United States is Mexico's largest trading partner along with Canada. This gives it a lot of influence in Mexico. It has always been concerned about Mexico's stability and in the last

Below: **The border crossing between Nuevo Laredo in Mexico and Laredo in the United States. Nuevo Laredo receives more daily visitors from the United States than any other border town.**

twenty years, has stepped in several times to help when Mexico has had problems with its economy. Mexicans usually have mixed feelings on these occasions, and periodically, Mexico has resisted control by the United States. In 1938, for example, Mexico nationalized oil production and kicked out a number of American companies. Mexico also refused to side with the United States in condemning Fidel Castro after the Cuban Revolution in 1959. Nevertheless, trade and cooperation have continued to expand, and relations are generally good.

Opposite: **National University in Mexico City. It offers special courses for foreigners, including Americans, who wish to learn Spanish or more about Mexico's history and culture.**

The Mexican–American War

Mexico and the United States were not always peaceful neighbors. In 1846, they went to war with each other. The state of Texas is what actually sparked the conflict. Texas was a part of Mexico until 1836, when in response to harsh restrictions placed on its population by Mexican General Santa Anna, Texas started the fight for its own independence. It was an independent republic for ten years until, under U.S. President James K. Polk, the U.S. Congress voted in 1845 to make Texas part of the United States. The United States did not initially want to include Texas as a state because Texans were slave-owners, and slavery was a very sensitive issue in the United States at that time. However, once they decided to include it, they wanted Mexico to agree that the southern boundary of Texas would be the Rio Grande River. They also wanted Mexico to sell present-day California and New Mexico to the United States. President Polk sent John Slidell to Mexico City to negotiate with the Mexicans, but the Mexican government refused to meet with Slidell. Polk ordered American troops to occupy the land between the Rio Grande and the Nueces River farther north in Texas. By April 1846, war had begun!

Below: The Alamo, San Antonio, Texas. A famous battle took place here in March 1836. The Texans defending it against Mexican troops were all killed. But the tide turned by April, and under the leadership of Sam Houston, Texans defeated the Mexican forces.

Left: The Mexican-American War broke out in 1846. U.S. troops easily captured California and New Mexico. When Mexico City was also captured, the Mexican government decided to negotiate peace.

The Defeat of Mexico

The war was a very uneven contest because the Americans had better trained and equipped soldiers and more sophisticated guns. The Mexicans had more soldiers, but most of them had no training and old-fashioned guns. The United States began a many-sided attack on Mexico, sending some troops to California and New Mexico, some south through Texas, and some by ship to the southern port of Veracruz on the eastern coast of Mexico. In March of 1847, General Winfield Scott landed at Veracruz and laid siege to the city. He took Veracruz despite very brave efforts by the Mexicans and occupied Mexico City in September of that year. The war ended, and the Mexicans had to agree to sell half their territory to the Americans for fifteen million dollars. The Americans left in May 1848 after signing an agreement called the Treaty of Guadalupe Hidalgo. Texas, California, New Mexico, Colorado, Nevada, Arizona, and areas of Wyoming and Utah all became part of the United States. Losing the war resulted in a strong feeling of resentment against the United States, which to some degree has continued to affect relations.

Above: General Antonio López de Santa Anna seized power in Mexico in 1833. He led the troops that were defeated first in Texas and then against the U.S. in the Mexican–American War.

NAFTA: A Free Trade Agreement

Today, the United States and Canada are Mexico's largest trading partners. NAFTA (North American Free Trade Agreement) is an agreement between the three countries of North America — Canada, the United States, and Mexico — to buy and sell food and other goods among themselves without charging one another extra taxes. This is known as free trade and went into effect in January of 1994. It is meant to make it easier for manufacturers to sell their products anywhere in North America without restrictions. It is also hoped that more jobs will result for everyone.

Above: **Carlos Salinas de Gortari was president of Mexico when the NAFTA deal was signed in 1992.**

NAFTA makes all three countries much stronger on the world economy since there is such a large market for their goods close to home. Although NAFTA is still new, it seems to be improving the economies of all three countries. This trade agreement also makes people realize how important each country is to the other and so improves relations. Mexico exports crude petroleum products, engines, electrical goods, and vegetables to the U.S. The U.S. exports car parts, industrial machinery, iron, steel, cereals, and chemicals to Mexico. Canada sends electronic and auto parts for assembly to Mexico and buys back the cars or electronic goods.

Below: **Mexico exports vegetables and fruits to the United States and Canada.**

Border Industries

Since the free trade agreement, industry along the Mexican–U.S. border has grown. There are many assembly plants called *maquiladoras* (mah-kee-lah-DOHR-ahs) in the border towns in Mexico, which make goods such as clothes, furniture, electronics, and automobile parts to sell to the United States and Canada. These industries are located in Mexico because it is cheaper to manufacture goods there. It benefits the American companies and also provides jobs to the Mexicans. However, there are also concerns because the maquiladoras employ mostly women who are poorly paid and work in bad conditions. The industries also attract more people than there are jobs. As a result, towns are filled with people looking for work, and many try to cross the border illegally into the United States.

Water and air pollution has also been a problem because of the high concentration of industries along the border. Some of the waterways became dangerously polluted by U.S. companies that, for many years, took advantage of the lower environmental restrictions in Mexico. However, as a result of NAFTA, an environmental plan has been created to improve water and air quality in the border region and clean up polluted areas.

Immigration to the United States

Many Mexicans have settled in the United States in the border states — in California, Texas, and in the southwest. Mexico is much poorer than the United States and has a growing population of people who cannot find work and who think life is better in the United States. These people have been migrating both legally and illegally to America throughout the twentieth century. There have been times when the United States has encouraged emigration from Mexico, but most of the time it is worried about the high numbers of Mexicans crossing the border every year to find work.

During World War II, the United States made it legal for Mexicans to emigrate since they needed workers to help make weapons and war materials. This was called the Bracero Program. Salaries in the United States were so much higher than in Mexico that many poor farmers at that time left their villages to work in the United States. But in 1964, American workers complained that American citizens could not get jobs. The program was ended, but immigration to the U.S. continues to the present day, often illegally.

Below: This U.S. patrol car is guarding the Mexican–American border. The shared border results in many poor Mexicans try to emigrate illegally to the United States. The U.S. government has a difficult time patrolling the long, isolated stretches along the Rio Grande and farther west.

Blending at the Borders

Many cities and towns along the Mexican–U.S. border have a life of their own and attract travelers and workers from both countries. American tourists often cross the border simply for the day to visit places such as Tijuana, near San Diego in California, or Nuevo Laredo, which is near Laredo and San Antonio in Texas. Some U.S. citizens who work in San Diego live in Tijuana. Others travel to Mexico simply to shop for cheap goods. Around Nuevo Laredo, people on both sides of the border celebrate the same holidays — whether it be Mexican Independence Day or Washington's Birthday. They even share a professional baseball team that plays in both countries' minor leagues!

Although many legal immigrants from Mexico build a successful life in the United States, most illegal immigrants live in very poor conditions. They may work as fruit-pickers in California or as sweatshop workers in cities such as Chicago and New York, where they get little pay. It is a difficult problem for the governments of the two countries. It is hoped that Mexico will be made stronger and richer through NAFTA, and that with a better future in Mexico, more people will choose to stay there.

Above: **Some familiar American characters for sale on the streets in Mexico — Mickey Mouse and Ernie. The influence of its large neighbor can be seen in various ways in Mexico. But Mexican culture has also had an effect in the United States, and Mexican food, movie stars, and music have all become popular in the U.S.**

Mexican-American Communities

There are large Mexican-American communities in the United States, particularly in the border states of Texas, California, and New Mexico. Mexican-American communities in cities such as San Antonio, Austin, and Los Angeles have kept many traditional Mexican customs and celebrations. The family, for instance, is still very important in Mexican-American culture. Most children have godparents, a good way of forming strong links with unrelated people in the community. *Machismo* (mah-chees-moh) is usually also important in these families — the idea that the men have to be very masculine and dominant in the household.

Many traditional Mexican festivals are celebrated every year in these cities — for example, you can see Day of the Dead, Cinco de Mayo, or Independence Day celebrations. In rural areas of the southwest and California, there are also local patron saint celebrations, similar to those held in Mexico. There are religious services and a parade of the saints around the village and fields, accompanied by a local band.

Below: **Mexican-American communities continue to celebrate traditional Mexican holidays in the U.S. This parade in New Mexico includes young ballet folklorico dancers. There may also be mariachi bands and traditional foods, including tamales and hot chocolate.**

Americans in Mexico

Many North Americans also visit Mexico, and some go to live there. Since the 1960s, Mexico has been a major tourist destination for Americans. Millions visit Mexico at least once, and some come back every year. Others retire in Mexico, particularly in Baja California and in Mexico City. Many Americans like Mexico because it is close to home and is much cheaper than many other travel destinations, such as Europe. American high school and university students also visit Mexico in large numbers to study Spanish or attend Mexico's universities.

Finally, with so much commerce between the two countries, some Americans come to live in Mexico to manage companies or buy and sell their goods. Artists are also attracted to the place. William Spratling, an American architect and professor, moved to Taxco in Mexico in 1929 and started a successful business in silver jewelry that drew on ancient Indian designs. His pieces were in high demand in the United States.

There are big differences between rich Americans coming to enjoy the beaches of Mexico and poor Mexicans trying to get work in the United States. But the extent of immigration in both directions means the two are closely connected in many ways.

Above: **Mexican beaches, such as those at Cancun, Cozumel, and Acapulco, draw many American tourists every year, particularly during the U.S. and Canadian winter months.**

Shooting to Fame

Many Mexicans as well as Mexican-Americans have become famous in the United States. Salma Hayek is a current star in the movie industry, and her beautiful looks have quickly made her a favorite in Hollywood. She was born in Veracruz, Mexico, to a Mexican mother and Lebanese father. She began her acting career in Mexican television soap operas. After moving to Los Angeles, her first big hit in Hollywood came with the release of *Desperado* in 1995. She went back to film other movies in Mexico but has recently become famous with the Hollywood production of *Fools Rush In*, released in 1997.

Anthony Quinn is another famous movie actor who was born in Mexico but moved to the United States. He has won two Oscars for Best Supporting Actor and has appeared in over two hundred films including the classic, *Zorba the Greek*. Linda Ronstadt and Joan Baez are folksingers with Mexican backgrounds. Linda Ronstadt, who is versatile in pop, rock, and folk music, went back to her roots and recorded Mexican ballads in the late 1980s.

Today, Rudy Galindo, born to Mexican-American parents in California, is skating his way into American hearts. He was the first Latino to win in the 1996 U.S. Men's Iceskating championship finals! He also went on to win the bronze medal in the World Championships held in Canada in 1996.

Below, left: **Anthony Quinn was born in 1915 in Chihuahua, Mexico. He moved to California at a young age. He is best known for his lead-role in the movie *Zorba the Greek* (1964); more recently he acted in *A Walk in the Clouds* (1995). Quinn is also a sculptor and painter.**

Below, right: **Salma Hayek has become a star in Hollywood.**

Sharing Cultures

With so much movement across the border, Mexican culture has had a big influence on the United States, as of course U.S. culture has had in Mexico. The traditional foods of America and Mexico, for example, can easily be found in both places. You can eat tacos and burritos in any major city of the United States and hamburgers in most major cities of Mexico. There is even a separate type of cooking that blends the two cultures' foods, called Tex-Mex. If you've ever eaten chile con carne, you've had Tex-Mex. All of the names used for Mexican dishes are in fact Spanish words, so you have been learning the language as well! Did you know that chile con carne means "chili with meat" in Spanish? And if you are in Mexico, to order a hamburger, you ask for a *hamburguesa* (ham-boor-GAY-sah). Mexican writers and artists are also becoming well known in the U.S. and Canada. Mexican soap operas are broadcast on American television in areas with a large number of Spanish-speaking people. You may have even grown up watching a Mexican mouse on Saturday morning television. Do you know "Speedy Gonzalez?" He speaks with a Mexican accent, and most of the cartoons portray Mexico! As you can see, there are many ways that Mexicans and Americans are trading ideas about how to live.

Above: **Does this food stand look like it is in Mexico? These enchiladas and juices are actually for sale in New Mexico, in the United States.**

LA BAMBA

American music is very popular with young people in Mexico, but Mexican music is popular in the United States, too! The Texas Tornadoes, for instance, play Tex-Mex music and have won a Grammy Award. "La Bamba," made famous by Los Lobos, is actually a Mexican folk song!

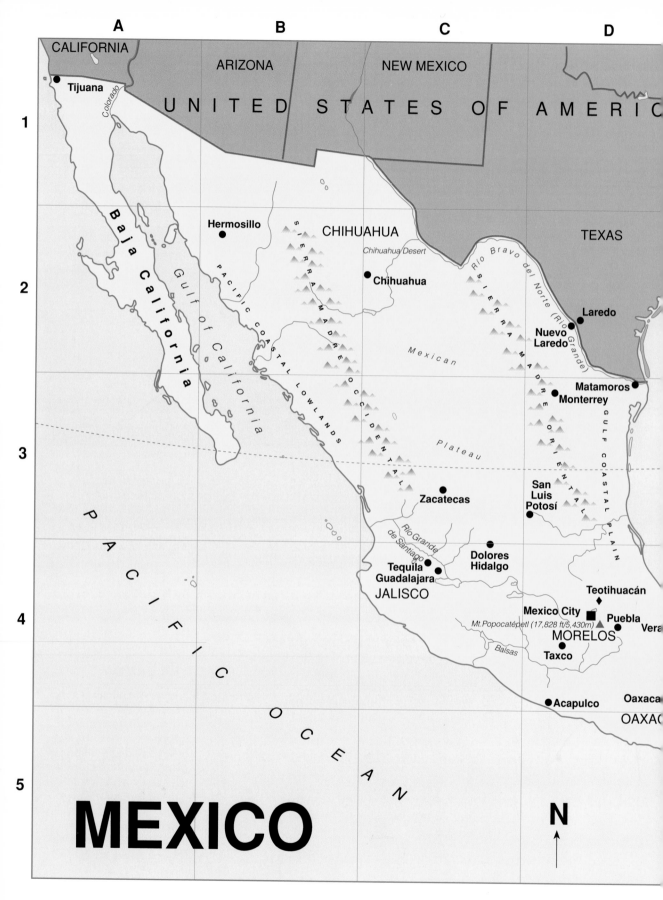

MEXICO

N

86

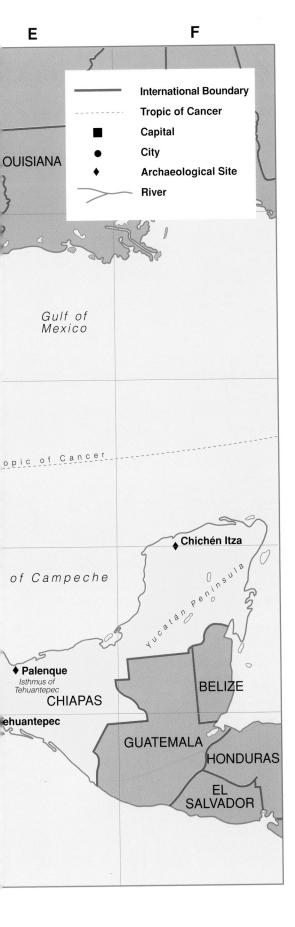

E   F

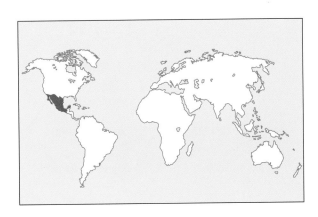

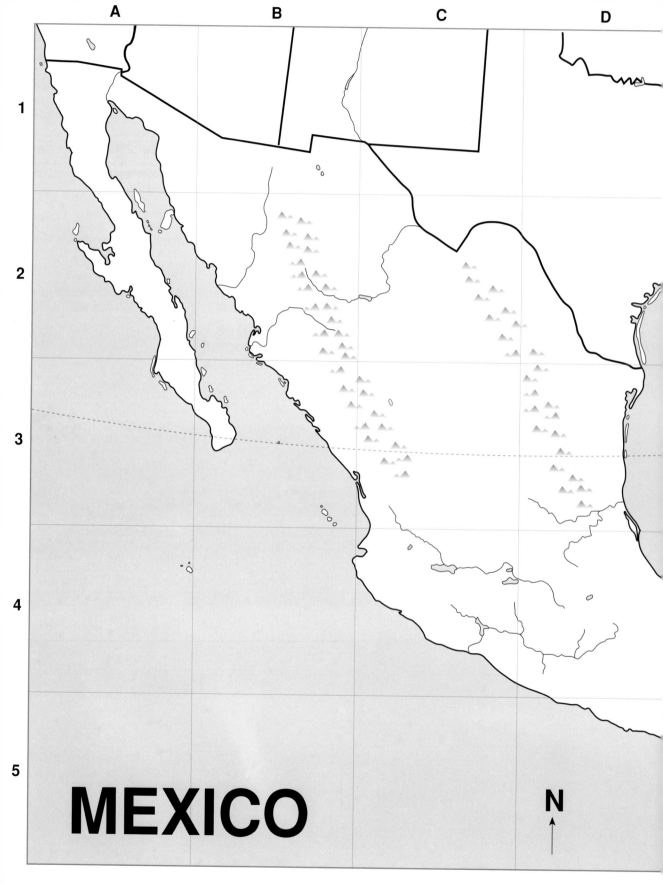

A   B   C   D

1

2

3

4

5

MEXICO

N

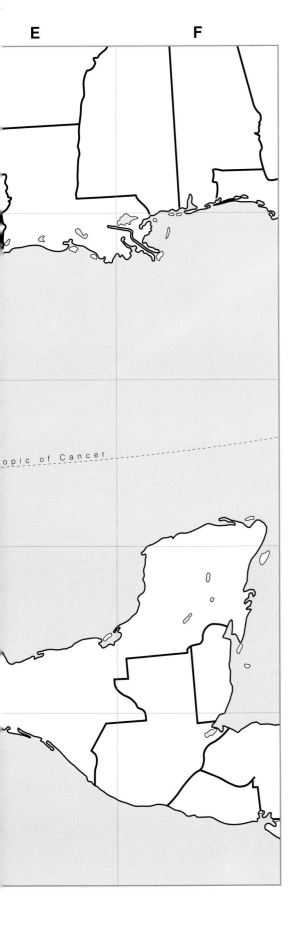

E F

opic of Cancer

How Is Your Geography?

Learning to identify the main geographical areas and points of a country can be challenging. Although it may seem difficult at first to memorize the location and spelling of major cities or the names of mountain ranges, rivers, deserts, lakes, and other prominent physical features, the end result of this effort can be very rewarding. Places you previously did not know existed will suddenly come to life when referred to in world news, whether in newspapers, television reports, or other books and reference sources. This knowledge will make you feel a bit closer to the rest of the world, with its fascinating variety of cultures and physical geography.

Used in a classroom setting, the instructor can make duplicates of this map using a copy machine (PLEASE DO NOT WRITE IN THIS BOOK!). Students can then fill in any requested information on their individual map copies. Used one-on-one, the student can also make copies of the map on a copy machine and use them as a study tool. The student can practice identifying place names and geographical features on his or her own.

Mexico at a Glance

Official Name   Estado Unidos Mexicanos; United Mexican States

Capital City   Mexico City

Independence   August 24, 1821

Current President   Ernesto Zedillo Ponce de León, elected in 1994

Mexican Revolution   1910–1920; new constitution approved 1917

Land Area   756,066 square miles; 1,958,210 square kilometers

Longest River   Río Bravo del Norte (Rio Grande)

Population   93,985,848 (1995 estimate)

Official Language   Spanish

States   Aguascalientes, Baja California Norte, Baja California Sur, Campeche, Chiapas, Chihuahua, Coahuila, Colima, Durango, Guanajuato, Guerrero, Hidalgo, Jalisco, Michoacán, Morelos, Nayarit, Nuevo León, Oaxaca, Puebla, Querétaro, Quintana Roo, San Luis Potosí, Sinaloa, Sonora, Tabasco, Tamaulipas, Tlaxcala, Veracruz, Yucatán, Zacatecas

Religion   Roman Catholic (93.5 percent); Protestant (4.9 percent); other (1.6 percent)

Historical Figures   Montezuma II; Hernán Cortés; Malinali; Father Hidalgo; Benito Juárez; Porfirio Díaz; Emiliano Zapata; Pancho Villa

Borders   United States, Guatemala, and Belize

Important Holidays   Epiphany (Three Kings Day), January 6
Birthday of Benito Juárez, March 21
Cinco de Mayo, May 5
Independence Day, September 15–16
Day of the Dead, November 1, 2
Feast of Our Lady of Guadalupe, December 12

Currency   Mexican Peso (8.3 pesos = U.S. $1 as of 1998)

Opposite: **In a daring performance, this man dives off high cliffs into the sea below in Acapulco.**

Glossary

Spanish Vocabulary

aguacate (ag-wah-KAH-tay): avocado.

buen provecho (boo-ayn pro-VAY-cho): "Enjoy your Meal."

calaveras (kah-lah-VAY-rahs): candies in the shape of skulls, used in Day of the Dead celebrations.

charreada (chah-ray-AH-dah): rodeo.

charros (CHAR-rohz): cowboys in Mexico.

chinampas (chee-NAHM-pahs): floating gardens around Tenochtitlán upon which the Aztecs grew food.

comal (KOH-mal): a flat clay dish for cooking tortillas.

comida (koh-MEE-dah): main meal eaten at midday.

compadres (kom-PAH-drays): godparents.

concheros (kon-CHAY-rohs): dancers in Aztec clothing who wear shells called *conchas* (KON-chahs) around their ankles.

curandero (koor-ahn-DAY-roh): Indian healer.

enchiladas (en-chee-LAH-dahs): soft tortillas filled with chili sauce and other delightful foods.

fiesta (fee-AY-stah): party or festival.

fútbol (FOOT-bohl): soccer.

guacamole (gwa-kah-MO-lay): a cold dish of mashed avocado with onion, tomato, chilies, and cilantro.

jugos (HOO-gohs): fresh juice.

mal ojo (mal OH-ho): evil eye; belief that some people can cause illness in others.

maquiladoras (mah-kee-lah-DOHR-ahs): factories located along the Mexico-U.S. border.

mariachi (mah-ree-AH-chee): type of Mexican music and band consisting of three violins, guitars, and two trumpets.

metate (may-TAH-tay): stone mill for grinding corn.

Mexica (mayk-SEE-kah): name of the tribe of Indians later known as Aztecs; source of the name Mexico.

norteña (nor-TAHN-ya): a common musical style in Mexico. It combines European musical influences with Mexican ballads and salsa. This style began in northern Mexico and southern parts of Texas.

pan de muerto (PAN DAY moo-EHR-toh): "bread of the dead" — it is baked for Day of the Dead celebrations.

panuchos (pan-OO-chos): soft tortillas filled with beans and fried.

piñata (peen-YAH-tah): a clay pot filled with candies and toys that children break open at parties.

pulque (POOL-kay): an alcoholic drink made from agave.

quesadillas (kay-sah-DEE-as): soft tortillas filled with cheese and fried.

Quince años (KEEN-say AHN-yos): the celebration of a girl's fifteenth birthday.

siesta (see-AY-stah): midday rest.

tamales (tah-Mah-lays): a popular dish of corn and meat wrapped in a corn husk and steamed.

toros (TOH-rohs): bulls.

tortillas (tor-TEE-yahz): flat corn pancakes.

English Vocabulary

alliance: to join another group or person in a common cause.

blockade: to close off and prevent entry or exit.

branding: marking cattle by burning or otherwise to indicate ownership.

cacao: the tree that produces beans used in making chocolate.

Chilango (chee-LAN-go): Spanish dialect spoken in south central Mexico and Mexico City.

Churrigueresque (choo-REE-ger-ESK): New World architectural style that emerged in the eighteenth century; similar to Baroque and very elaborate.

coiling: making pots out of long strips of clay.

commemorate: to honor the memory of some event.

compulsory: required.

dialect: a variety of a language that differs from the standard language used.

Huitzilopochtli (hweet-seel-POSH-tlee): Aztec god of the sun.

illiteracy: the inability to read and write.

intricate: complex.

isolated: a place or community that is far from any other place or community.

lasso: a long rope with a noose at one end for roping cattle and horses.

matador: a bullfighter.

Mesoamerica: Middle America including Mexico and Central America.

mestizos (may-STEE-sos): people of mixed Indian and Spanish blood; the majority of Mexico's population.

missionary: a person sent by a church to convert others to his or her religion.

Montezuma (mon-tay-ZOO-mah): name of two Aztec kings; Montezuma II was king when the Spaniards arrived.

murals: large paintings on walls.

Nahuatl (nah-WAH-tul): language of the Aztec Indians.

Norteño (nor-TAYN-yo): Spanish dialect spoken in northern Mexico, along the border with the United States.

patron: a person or government who supports cultural efforts such as the arts.

peasant: a poor farmer.

pilgrim: a person who makes a long journey to a sacred religious site as an act of devotion.

pre-Columbian: the cultures present before the arrival of Columbus and European settlers to the Americas.

quetzal: a beautiful green bird of Mexico and Central America. The male has long, green tail feathers.

Quetzalcoatl (KAYT-sal-koh-AT-ul): Aztec god of wind and breath; believed to be a feathered snake.

repressive: something that keeps others in check, suppressing behavior and opinions.

silversmith: a person who makes or repairs pieces of silver.

Tenochtitlán (tay-NOSH-teet-lan): capital city of the Aztecs; located at the same site as modern-day Mexico City.

vendor: a person or stand that has items for sale.

Yucateco (yoo-ka-TAY-ko): Spanish dialect spoken on the Yucatán Peninsula.

Zapatistas: peasants from the state of Chiapas who started a rebellion in 1994.

More Books to Read

The Ancient Maya. Cultures of the Past series. Irene Flum Galvin (Marshall Cavendish)

The Aztecs. Tim Wood (Hamlyn Children's Books)

The Aztecs. Footsteps in Time series. Sally Hewitt (Children's Press)

Children of the Sierra Madre. Frank Staub (Carolrhoda Books)

Children of Yucatán. Frank Staub (Carolrhoda Books)

Coming to America: the Mexican-American Experience. Elizabeth Martinez (The Milbrook Press)

Days of the Dead. Kathryn Lasky (Hyperion Books for Children)

Fiesta: Mexico's Great Celebrations. Elizabeth Silverthorne (Mullbrook Press)

Mexico. Festivals of the World series. Elizabeth Berg (Gareth Stevens)

Miguel Hidalgo y Costilla: Father of Mexican Independence. Frank De Varona (The Milbrook Press)

Traditional Crafts from Mexico and Central America. Florence Temko (Lerner Publications)

Videos

The Buried Mirror: Reflections on Spain and the New World. Carlos Fuentes (Sogetel with the Smithsonian Institution)

Fodor's Video Mexico. (a co-production of TravelWorld Video and J. Mitchell Johnson Productions)

Imagining New Worlds. (BBC for the Open University)

Web Sites

www.mexonline.com/

www.realtime.com/maya/index.html

www.ilap.com/~tgmag/ap/apmex.html

Due to the dynamic nature of the Internet, some web sites stay current longer than others. To find additional web sites, use a reliable search engine with one or more of the following keywords to help you locate information about Mexico. Keywords: *Mexico, Mexicans, Aztecs, Hernán Cortés, Diego Rivera, Maya, charros.*

Index